The Yorkshire Terrier

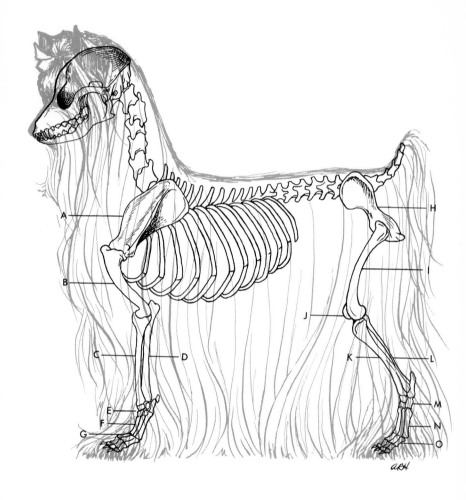

A— Scapula

B— Humerus

C— Radius

D— Ulna

E— Carpus

F— Metacarpus

G— Phalanges

H— Ilium

I— Femur

J— Patella

K— Tibia

L— Fibula

M—Tarsus

N—Metatarsus

O— Phalanges

THE YORKSHIRE TERRIER

Origin, History and Complete Care

Aileen Markley Martello

AN EXPOSITION-BANNER BOOK

Exposition Press   *New York*

The author's Yorkshire Terriers shown in the
book and on the jacket were photographed by
Stubbings Studio, Lancaster, California

E X P O S I T I O N   P R E S S   I N C .

50 Jericho Turnpike   Jericho, New York 11753

F I R S T   E D I T I O N

LIBRARY OF CONGRESS CATALOG CARD NUMBER: 74-146912

0-682-47245-X

Dedicated to my husband Joe,
a kind and patient man,
who does love Yorkies.

Contents

Preface

This book was written in the hope that it will assist and guide the novice breeder of the Yorkshire Terrier. The beginning breeder too often is neglected and ignored, although it is from the ranks of these beginners that the serious breeders of the future will emerge.

It is difficult to obtain written information on Yorkshire Terriers because they were not a popular breed until recently. Little was published about them except for an occasional chapter in books on all breeds of dogs, and these scant references are difficult to find.

It is essential that the novice breeder has some knowledge of the breed and knows its history in order to encamp on a successful breeding program. It is the purpose of this book to start you on your way. It is written in simple, easy to understand terms intended as a ready reference. It is factual, with knowledge gathered from years of research, experience and information passed on to me from older breeders. Instructions on care, feeding and grooming have been approved by my veterinarian and other authorities on the breed. The names of dogs and kennels mentioned are to be found in early and present-day pedigrees. The pictures are of people who have earned for themselves a place in the development and continued improvement of the breed. Many of the illustrations are collectors' items that a novice would not have access to; others are of outstanding Yorkies in today's pedigrees.

Special thanks go to my dear friends Indie Rice, Goldie Stone and Edith Stirk, who gave me inspiration and unstinting aid, to Anne Reitz Holt, whose beautiful illustrations were a labor of love and real help to me, and to Dr. James J. Sloan, an exceptionally dedicated veterinarian on whom I have leaned heavily for medical advice, and who has guided my breeding program throughout the years.

AILEEN MARKLEY MARTELLO

The Yorkshire Terrier

CHAPTER 1

Origin and History of the Breed

Dog books published in England as early as 1884 tell us that the Yorkshire Terrier is a man-made breed of dog. The authors of these books always state that the exact origin of the breed is a mystery, since no written records were kept of the pedigrees of the original breed crossings nor were dates of breedings recorded.

These authors believed that the breed was begun in the early 1800's by people with a sound knowledge of breeding and a preconceived idea of what they were eventually going to produce. It was no accident, then, that small, long-haired dogs emerged from a combination breeding of large dogs with soft, silky hair, large dogs with short, wiry hair and medium-sized dogs with long hair. We can only guess at the breeds used in obtaining the final results.

All available records show that the first Yorkie-type dogs originated in Yorkshire and Lancashire among the working-class men of the wool mills. Many old-timers claim that these breeders were Paisley weavers who had come down from Scotland during the Industrial Revolution of those days and settled in the area, bringing their dogs with them. From the original, rough type, they interbred them to the point where they would breed true to the type originally planned. Many such breeders had to work on the problem since it would have been impossible for all of them to have used exactly the same out-crossings. Transportation was difficult and the mill workers had little time to travel.

These men had few luxuries and their dogs were a great part of their lives. The men would meet at local pubs and take their dogs along to show competitively. Checking progress in breeding at these times, they undoubtedly interbred with some of their own strains. Rivalry must have been fierce among them; this could be another reason why no written records were kept.

Many early authors say that the breed was probably made from crossing and recrossing the Black and Tan Broken-Haired Scotch Terrier, the Paisley or Clydesdale Terrier, the Maltese, the Dandie Dinmont and the Skye Terrier. Others state that it was merely a

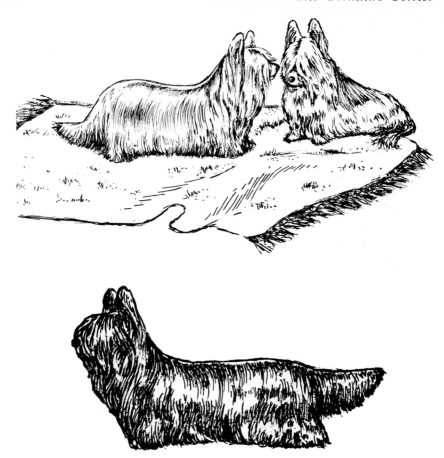

Clydesdale (or Paisley) Terriers.

cross between the silky-coated Skye Terrier and the old Broken-Haired Scotch Terrier, who is the foundation of so many of the present-day long-haired dogs.

In *The Dog Book* by James Watson (1905), published by Doubleday, Page and Company, New York, the author states his opinion that the Airedale and the Yorkshire Terrier are from the same parent stock, a medium-sized, grizzle and tan Terrier common in Yorkshire and within the memory of the oldest inhabitant and even some of the younger ones. He backs up this opinion with an illustration, a picture of a dog named Bounce which appeared in Stonehenge's first edition of *Dogs of the British Isles* and was captioned "Dogs not being Skyes, Dandies, foxes or toys." The picture was in the introductory chapter on Terriers. The same illustration appeared as a frontispiece in the second edition of 1872. Bounce was the Halifax Terrier, the blue-tan Terrier that Peter Eden of Manchester had at that time. The caption under the picture reads "Original Yorkshire Terrier"—"The Broken-Haired Terrier"—"A Specimen Dog of Mrs. Radcliffe's Breeding" and "The Smooth Black and Tan Terrier." In this illustration Bounce is even larger than the Broken-Haired Terrier and appears to have a short, rough coat. Mr. Watson also states, "If Bounce was an improved Terrier from the common run, what could his progenitors have been like, say in 1840?"

There is little doubt that the Paisley or Clydesdale Terrier was part of the original cross, but whether he or the Yorkshire-type came first will never be known for sure. The Clydesdale was never popular, since it was extremely difficult to breed him to meet his standard. This standard was written before that of the Yorkshire Terrier and was evidently used to formulate the original Yorkshire standard, since the two are similar on so many points.

Another point of confusion was that the Scotch people never admitted the true origin of the Clydesdale or Paisley Terrier. This breed was a subject of great controversy during the 1870's when breeders were trying to disentangle the different breeds of so-called Scotch Terriers, who had been lumped in one mass for showing. This controversy eventually separated several breeds and each was given a separate classification in shows and stud books. The Clydesdale or Paisley Terrier was one of the principal characters in this comedy of errors and was described as an anomaly. He finally ended up being classified as a non-sporting dog. At the same time he was said to be a cross between the Skye Terrier and the Yorkshire Terrier. With information like this, written by authors and appearing on dog records in the 1870's, we wonder which came first, the chicken or the egg.

Breeds were not carefully classified in early dog shows, and records show that Yorkshire-type dogs were being shown as early as 1860 and listed for show as Toy Terriers, Scotch Terriers with Cut Ears, Scotch Terriers with Dropped Ears, Blue-Fawn Terriers, Broken-Haired Terriers and Rough and Broken-Haired Terriers. Even these classes were divided by weight. Yorkshire-type dogs continued to be shown under all of these classifications for many years, but they finally were given a separate place in the *Stud Book* of 1862. The first published issue of the *Stud Book*, in 1874, listed them as "Broken-Haired or Yorkshire Terriers." Until the

Stud Book of 1886 they were never mentioned as merely "York-shire Terriers," so the English Kennel Club did not give them separate recognition until that time. To add to the confusion, early stud books listed the dogs merely by call name and with no pedigree. Comparatively few dogs were registered in any breed at that time, so people evidently felt that the dog was well known and needed no pedigree or background.

In December, 1869, the great Huddersfield Ben made his first public appearance at a show in Manchester. Ben was bred by Mr. Eastwood of Huddersfield and was owned and shown to fame by Mrs. Jonas Foster of Bradford. Ben's life was short but productive; he had won over 100 prizes before his untimely death in a road accident at the age of six and a half years.

Knowledgeable people have always considered Ben the "Father of the Yorkshire Terrier" as we know him today. Ben was an extremely prepotent sire who did much to stabilize the breed by passing on so many of his good qualities and characteristics to his offspring. His sons and daughters were the foundations of most of the good old strains of Yorkies in England. Ben was also considered to be the greatest stud dog in England in his day.

Ben's pedigree is of interest to all of us today since it shows, to some extent, the breeding that was done to produce him. His pedigree has vacant spots in it for us to wonder about, but it is the oldest known pedigree on record for a Yorkshire Terrier. The pedigree is listed in the *English Kennel Club Stud Book* of 1874 with the number 3612. The pedigree was listed in this old form:

THE PEDIGREE OF HUDDERSFIELD BEN

By Mr. Boscovitch's dog out of *Lady*, his sire by Thomas Ramsden's *Bounce*, by his *Bob* out of his *Old Dolly*. *Bob* by *Haigh's Teddy* (from Lascelles Hall, Huddersfield) out of *Old Dolly*. *Teddy* by J. Swift's *Old Crab* (from Manchester) out of Kershaw's *Old Kitty* (from Halifax). *Lady* by Eastwood's *Old Ben*, and granddaughter of *Old Sandy*. *Ben* by Ramsden's *Bounce* out of *Young Dolly*, by *Old Sandy* out of *Old Dolly*, by *Albert* (from Manchester), by *Old Soldier*. *Old Sandy* by *Haigh's Teddy* out of Walshaw's *Kitty*, by the Healy House dog, out of Walshaw's *Pink*.

To study this pedigree, copy it onto a present-day pedigree form. Ben's pedigree has much to tell us about the dogs of his day and about linebreeding. His great-great-grandsire on his sire's side is Haigh's Teddy and Teddy's sire is J. Swift's Old Crab, who is on record as being a long-haired Black and Tan Terrier. Teddy's dam, Kershaw's Old Kitty, was listed as a drop-eared Skye-type Terrier. Old Kitty had been stolen in Manchester and eventually became the property of Mr. J. Kershaw, who successfully bred her.

Notice that Old Crab and Old Kitty were identified by their names, the name of their owners and a description of the type of dog they were. Neither one was called a Yorkshire-type dog, as so many were at this time who were being shown. (Albert from Manchester, who appears in Ben's pedigree, was being shown at this time and was listed as a Yorkshire-type dog.) Someone took the time to describe these two dogs, and the description may be found in many old books, but nowhere is there a description of any of the other dogs in the same generation as Old Crab and Old Kitty except for Albert, who is mentioned as the Yorkshire-type.

Evidently, the fact that these dogs are mentioned often causes the mistaken idea that Old Crab and Old Kitty are the origin of the Yorkshire Terrier. This statement is untrue, as is the statement that Mr. Peter Eden was the "Inventor of the Yorkshire Terrier." Mr. Eden was noted for his Pugs and Bulldogs. He was certainly one of the earliest owners and breeders of Yorkies, but he was known to have purchased most of them from the workingmen in Lancashire. Later he bred them. Albert was only one of the Yorkies with which Mr. Eden convinced the public of the charm of the breed.

Mr. Eden may have given the breed its first impulse, but Mrs. Jonas Foster was for years the center of all Yorkie activity and it was undoubtedly she who raised the variety to its highest point of perfection up to this time. Her Yorkies were kept in excellent condition; she never exhibited a poor specimen. Her Huddersfield Ben, Toy Smart, Bright, Sandy, Ted, Bradford Hero, Bradford Kate and her tinies were remembered for their uniform excellence. Her Ch. Ted was the winner of 267 first prizes and his name appeared in many of the bloodlines of the early Yorkies. Aside from breeding and showing top quality Yorkies for many years, Mrs. Foster was the first woman to judge dogs at any show in England. She made her debut at Leeds in 1889.

In 1968 the oldest known living breeder of Yorkies in England was quoted as saying that he had started to show them in 1900.

At that time the breed was said to have been made from the Scottish Terrier, hence the occasional harsh coat; the Black and Tan Terrier, for the tan; the Skye Terrier, to try to improve the coat and finally, the Maltese, to get a more silky coat.

In the 1800's the Maltese breed also was still a mixed one. One called Maltese was very small and had a curly coat. This type of Maltese is said to be the ancestor of the Bichon Frise, recognized as a breed in France many years ago. The other so-called Maltese was slightly larger, had a straight coat and evidently was the ancestor of the present-day Maltese. These two types of dogs had been brought to England by officers and sailors who were stationed on the Isle of Malta.

Reading and studying the statements of these early authors, we can see some reason for the many changes that take place in our breed from the time they are puppies until they are mature dogs. Also, we find reasons for throwbacks that unexpectedly appear in breeding Yorkies.

a. HOLT

CHAPTER 2

Famous Yorkies and Breeders
of England—Past and Present

During World War II many old books were destroyed in England. I was fortunate to be able to read and copy a few chapters for you to give you the different opinions of authors in their day.

Rawson B. Lee wrote a book titled *Terriers*. This was one volume of a set of books published in England in 1894. His chapter on Yorkshire Terriers reads as follows:

The late Peter Eden of Manchester, so noted in his day for pugs and bulldogs, owned Albert, a particularly good Yorkie. Albert had natural drop-ears, and with this variety ear cropping has increased and may now be said to be general. The Yorkie as a rule has his ears cut, and it is many years since I saw a really first-rate dog on the bench which had not been so mutilated. At the earlier shows excellent specimens appeared with their ears entire, and for them special classes were provided.

Actual measurements go for not very much, but length of the hair on the body and head of some of the best dogs is almost incredible, and its texture and color are simply extraordinary. It is said that when in his best form, the little dog Conqueror, owned by Mrs. Troughear of Leeds, had hair of almost uniform length of 24 inches; he weighed about 5½ pounds. One of the smartest little dogs of the variety, and a game little chap, was Mr. Kirby's Smart, who did a lot of winning about 20 years ago. Old Huddersfield Ben was another of the "pillars of the breed"; Mrs. Troughear's Dreadnought was another celebrity; Mrs. Foster's Bradford Bright and Sandy were notable dogs a few years ago. To the latter (one of our few lady judges) and her husband, Mr. Jonas Foster, more than to anyone else is due any little popularity the Yorkie possesses today. They have bred them for years and have from time to time owned the most perfect specimens imaginable. Mrs. Foster's Ted, who weighed 5 pounds, perhaps for all-round excellence never was excelled, and it was extremely funny to see this little whippet of a dog competing against an enormous St. Bernard or dignified bloodhound for the cup for the best animal in the show. Nor did the award always go to the big and the strong. One of the tiniest dogs I ever saw was one of Mrs. Foster's, shown at Westminster Aquarium in 1893, Mite, by name and nature, for it weighed a couple of pounds, was nicely formed, of fair color and quite as active as some of the bigger creatures brought into the ring, which they certainly did not grace. Another diminutive Yorkie is Mrs. Vaughan Fowler's Longbridge Bat, who weighs 2¾ pounds and is particularly smart and lively.

The best of the variety are certainly kept in a few hands. Among the older breeders were, in addition, Mr. John Inman, of Brighouse, Yorkshire; Mr. J. Spink, Bradford; Mr. A. Boulton, Accrington; Miss Alderson, Leeds; Mr. Cavanaugh, Leeds; Mr. Greenwood, Bradford; Mrs. Bligh Monck, Coley-Park, Reading; Lady Gifford, Redhill; and Mr. Wilkinson, Halifax; whilst the best modern kennels are those of Mrs. Foster, at Bradford; Mrs. Vaughan Fowler, Longbridge, Warwick; Mr. J. B. Leech, Clifton, Bristol; Mr. T. D. Hogson, Halifax; and Messrs. Walton and Beard, West Brompton.

The Yorkie is by no means a common commodity, and although third or fourth rate specimens are sometimes obtained from the London dealers, Bradford is their home. Here it is not difficult to obtain a suitable dog at a fair price.

On one occasion when the late Mr. E. Sandell required 3 or 4 of them for a certain purpose and was unable to obtain them in London, he would give a prize of a sovereign or two for the best Yorkie to be exhibited at a certain public-house on a certain evening. In due course a rare good collection was brought together from which the enterprising promoter speedily selected and purchased what he required, at the same time suiting himself, pleasing the dog-fanciers and, as it was said at the time, "doing a good turn for the publican."

Other comments regarding breeders and their Yorkies appear in a book published in London in 1907 and edited by Robert Leighton. In his chapter on the Yorkshire Terrier he mentions Mr. Peter Eden's Albert as one of the fine specimens and notes Mrs. Jonas Foster, whose success was due to her enthusiasm, the admirable condition in which her pets were always maintained and the care she bestowed on their toilets.

Her Ben, Toy Smart, Bright, Sandy, Ted, Bradford Hero, Bradford Marie, and Bradford Queen are remembered for their uniform excellence, Marie being a bitch weighing only 24 ounces. Mrs. Troughear's Conqueror and Dreadnought; Mr. Kirby's Smart; Mrs. Vaughan Fowler's Longbridge Bat, Bob and Daisy; and many others bred or owned by Mrs. Bligh Monck, Lady Gifford, Miss Alderson and Mr. Abraham Bolton, were prominent in the early days. Of more recent examples that have appeared and approached perfection may be mentioned Mrs. Walton's Ashton King, Ashton Queen and Bright and her Mont Thabor Duchess. Ashton Queen was said to have won more prizes than any other Yorkie living at that time. She was a granddaughter of Mrs. Foster's Ch. Ted and a daughter of his son Halifax Marvel.

Ch. Ashton Queen. A pillar of the breed and a rare portrait. She was shown around 1897.

Queen was whelped in 1892 or 1893 and an old print of her was found in an antique shop in England in 1969 and is reproduced in this book.

Mr. Leighton also mentions Mr. Mitchell's Westbrook Fred,

who won many honors, Mrs. Firmstone's Grand Duke and Mynd Damaris, and Mrs. Sinclair's Marcus Superbus, who stood high in the estimation of expert judges. There was another, perhaps the most beautiful bitch ever shown:

Her name was Waveless, the property of Mrs. R. Marshall, who is at present the owner of another admirable bitch named Little Picture. It is hazardous to pronounce an opinion upon the relative merits of dogs, but one has the support of many experts saying that the best all-round Yorkshire Terrier now living is Mrs. V. Shaw's Ch. Sneinton Amethyst, who has the merit of possessing a coat of excellent color and texture, not abnormally long, and who, in addition to his personal beauty, shows a desirable amount of that Terrier disposition which is happily being restored to the breed. Dogs are usually superior to bitches in type and substance, notwithstanding that many are unfortunately marred by imperfect mouths.

In France and Germany the Yorkshire Terrier has become the most popular lap-dog, sharing this distinction with the King Charles and other *chiens de luxe au d'agrement*. At the exhibition of dogs held in the Tuileries Gardens in May, 1907, there were 15 entries of Yorkies, prominent bitches being Royale-Beaute, Mont Thabor, Avent and Gamine. (Winners were placed in the order mentioned.) The dog winners were Mont Thabor Teddy, Royal Ideal and Tiny, who were judged by Mr. F. Gresham.

Following Mr. Leighton's chapter on Yorkies are pictures of Mrs. William Shaw's Ch. Sneinton Amethyst (by Ch. Ashton Duke ex Jackson's Vic), weighing 3 lbs. 2 oz. and of Mr. C. E. Firmstone's Mynd Damaris, Mynd Idol and The Grand Duke. The third picture is of Mrs. M. A. White's Sensation (by Grindley Superb ex Nan).

The Yorkies in these pictures were top Yorkies of their day and in excellent condition. They all had small, erect ears and long, flowing coats and the pictures, although black and white, showed clearly two definite colors in each dog's coat. All coats were much longer than we see them in the ring today. These are the Yorkies who were always wrapped, wore boots and were shown on their boxes. They would have difficulty walking in the rings of today because of the excess length of their coats.

These two articles are extremely important for the record of the breed since they prove that tiny Yorkies and Yorkies with length of coat were the top specimens of their day. Many people today are of the opinion that all Yorkies were large specimens with short coats until about thirty years ago. These writings prove that the size, color, type and texture of coat was set in the breed many years ago. However, it also proves that the tiny ones with the extreme wealth of coat and color were rare then, as they are today.

Until World War II broke out in England the average registration of Yorkies with the Kennel Club was about 250 per year. But then dog shows were discontinued and breeding almost stopped. Registrations dropped until in 1940 there were only 40 Yorkies registered and the breed was in danger of becoming extinct. From that year on registrations picked up, until today they are at an all-time high. In 1968 Yorkies had risen to number three on the list of all registered breeds and they were number one in breeds exported.

The last year before shows were discontinued, Ch. Delite of Invincia, bred by Mrs. Swan, was the last male champion to be made up and Ch. Benedetta of Soham was the last bitch to gain her championship. In 1947 shows started again and Ch. Ben's Blue Pride, bred by Mr. Roper, was the first new champion. The following years produced Ch. Wee Don of Atherleigh, bred by Mr. Hayes; Ch. McKay of Achmonie, bred by Miss MacDonald; Ch. Vemair Principal Boy, bred by Mr. Bain; Ch. Sorreldene Honey Son of the Vale, bred by Mrs. Sharpe; Ch. Wee Blue Atom, bred by Mr. Latliffe; Ch. Jessica of Westridge, bred by Mr. Grist; Ch. Butibel Perseus, bred by Mrs. Russell and Ch. Hampark Dandy, bred by Mr. Wilkinson.

This brings us to the present-day famous Yorkies and breeders, whose bloodlines and names appear in many American pedigrees today. Some champions were made up nearly twenty years ago but all were made after 1947, and all of these breeders or owners are credited with several famous champions.

Mrs. Annie Swan bred Ch. Splendour of Invincia, Ch. Sunstar of Invincia, Ch. Adora of Invincia, Ch. Titania of Invincia, Ch. Hopwood's Camelia, Ch. Stirkean's Chota Sahib and Ch. Dee Bee's Martini.

Mr. A .H. Coates owned or bred Ch. Blue Dolly, Ch. Martynwyn's Surprise of Atherleigh, Ch. Martynwyn's Adora and Ch.

Ch. Stirkean's Chota Sahib, top; Ch. Stirkean's Mr. Tims, bottom; both famous English studs.

Martynwyn's Debonaire. Much of the Coates' stock came to the United States and Canada during this time.

Mrs. M. U. Crookshank owned or bred Ch. Medium of Johnstounburn, Ch. Tufty of Johnstounburn, Ch. Myrtle of Johnstounburn, Ch. Pipit of Johnstounburn, Ch. Pimbron of Johnstounburn and Ch. Mr. Pim of Johnstounburn, who was her most famous champion.

Mrs. Ethel Munday and Miss Vera Munday owned or bred Ch. Midnight Gold of Yadnum, Ch. Eoforwic Envoy of Yadnum, Ch. Elmsglade Galahad of Yadnum, Ch. Moonglow of Yadnum, Ch. Gold Button of Yadnum and Ch. Luna Star of Yadnum. Mrs. Munday has many champions on the Continent and in America today.

Mrs. Edith A. Stirk owned or bred Ch. Titania of Invincia, Ch. Stirkean's Chota Sahib, Ch. Stirkean's Kandy Boy, Ch. Stirkean's Mr. Tims, Ch. Stirkean's Dee Bee's Faustina, Ch. Stirkean's Astonoff's Horatio, Ch. Stirkean's Rhapsody, Ch. Stirkean's Reenie, Ch. Stirkean's Gerrard's Little Guy and also many champions in America, Germany and Sweden.

Mrs. S. D. Beech owned or bred Ch. Dee Bee's Martini, Ch. Dee Bee's Hot Toddy, Ch. Stirkean's Dee Bee's Faustina, Ch. Dee Bee's Campari, Ch. Dee Bee's Isa la Bella, Ch. Dee Bee's Gold Fleck, Ch. Dee Bee's Gold Penny and Ch. Dee Bee's Doncella. During the past 12 years Mrs. Beech has finished 11 champions, most of them homebred. She showed her famous Faustina to a record which still stands in England today. Faustina won 23 bitch-Challenge Certificates; this is a record for any bitch. Mrs. Beech also has many champions in the rings today on the Continent.

Mrs. Marie Burfield owned or bred Ch. Buranthea's Doutelle, Ch. Buranthea's Angel Bright, Ch. Buranthea's Lucious Lady and Ch. Buranthea's St. Malachy. Many of her Yorkies are now in America and Japan.

Mrs. Connie Hutchin owned or bred Ch. Coulgorm Chloe, Ch. Don Carlos of Progresso, Ch. Progress of Progresso, Ch. Progresso Lover Boy, Ch. Progresso Prospect and Ch. Progresso Pearl. Most of these champions, along with other stock, are either in America or Japan today.

The past ten years have seen such a rise in popularity for the Yorkies that many more Challenge Certificates are issued each year and many lovely champions are made up. I am sorry that I have to omit so many of their names and their breeders' names.

Following is a list of English breeders with their prefixes. Some of these breeders are deceased, some are current-day breeders and some are new in the breed and got their start from the older breeders, but during the past 50 years each person mentioned has distinguished himself in the breed one way or another. The names and prefixes will give many American novices an insight into their pedigrees.

ATHERLEIGH—Mr. W. M. Hayes
BEECHRISE—Mrs. Les Griffiths
BLUESHEEN—Mrs. A. G. Bishop
BRIDLE—Mrs. M. Riley
BURANTHEA—Mrs. Marie Burfield
BURGHWALLIS—Mrs. M. Betton
BUTIBEL—Mrs. Jay Russell
CARLWYN—Mrs. W. E. Nicholls
CHANTMARLE—Mrs. Mary Hayes
CHARLEVIEW—Mr. George Tompkin
CLU MOR—Misses M. and F. Loton
CORIANDER—Mrs. L. Jones
COULGORM—Mr. A. Hughes
DEE BEE—Mrs. S. D. Beech
EASTGROVE—Mrs. V. Hargreaves
EOFORWIC—Mrs. M. Prosser
EPPERSTONE—Mrs. F. A. Furley
ERLCOUR—Mrs. E. Batsford
GERARDENE—Mrs. G. Anger
GLOAMIN'—Mrs. Emma Wilkinson
GOODIFF—Mr. M. Taylor
HEYTESBURY—Mr. J. O. O'Toole
HOPWOOD—Mrs. S. Myers
INVINCIA—Mrs. Annie Swan
JACARANDA—Mrs. J. Montgomery
JOHNSTOUNBURN—Mrs. M. U. Crookshank
KELSBRO—Mrs. H. Cross
LAMSGROVE—Mrs. Eva Lamb
LILACTIME—Mrs. Violet Howgill
LILYHILL—Mrs. Lowrie
MACSTROUD—Mr. David Stroud
MARTYNWYN—Mr. A. H. Coates
MUROSE—Mrs. E. Burton

PAGNELL—Mrs. S. I. Groom
PARKVIEW—Mr. William Bain
PHIRNO—Miss Phyllis Noakes
PHYLRENE—Mrs. F. C. Raine
PLANTATIONHALL—Mrs. Palframan
POMEROYWOOD—Mrs. Helen Wood
POOKSHILL—F. M. Wood
PRETORIA—A. Ross Buckley
PROGRESSO—Mrs. Connie Hutchin
SEHOW—Miss M. Howes
SOHAM—Lady Edith Windham-Dawson
SORRELDENE—Mrs. G. M. Bradley
STIRKEAN—Mrs. Edith Stirk
STREAMGLEN—Mrs. Mary Waldram
SUPREME—Mrs. E. Smith
TEMPLEVALE—Mrs. L. H. Briggs
TZUMIAO—Mrs. Elsie Gilbert
VALE—Mrs. Marjorie Nunn
VEMAIR—Mrs. V. M. Mair
WADEHOLME—Mrs. L. J. Wade
WESTRIDGE—Mrs. L. Grist
WHISPERDALE—Mr. R. Wardill
WINPAL—Miss E. A. Palmer
WISKE—Mrs. K. M. Renton
YADNUM—Mrs. Ethel and Miss Vera Munday
YORKFOLD—Mrs. Diane Rossiter

The past five years have brought many changes to the English show rings. Some well-known breeders and exhibitors have died while others have been ill, breeding few Yorkies and being unable to show the dogs they did breed. Many of their Yorkies were sold abroad during this period. The names of newer exhibitors, breeders and kennels can be traced to the stock of the older breeders, but now the new, serious breeders are developing their own strains.

CHAPTER 3

Early Yorkies in America—
Their Breeders and Fanciers

The Rawson B. Lee book *Terriers* contains one reference to Yorkies in America at that time (1894). Mr. Lee states that there is a record of Mrs. Troughear of Leeds selling her little dog Conqueror to Mrs. Emmott, who was the wife of an American actor. Conqueror was sold for £250. Evidently this dog came to America in the 1890's, and the value of the English pound then being much higher than it is today, this was a top price to be paid for a relatively unknown breed of dog.

Robert Leighton's book, published in 1907, is now the property of the Kennel Club in London. It contains a short reference to Yorkies in America at that time. The author states that attempts have frequently been made to establish the Yorkshire Terrier in America and that some choice specimens were exported there, but the climatic conditions appeared to be detrimental to most of the long-coated breeds. Among the American fanciers mentioned are Mrs. Raymond Malloch, who owned many good examples of the breed, and Mrs. Thomas, who did much to make the variety popular during the past years. These ladies succeeded to some extent in overcoming the difficulties of the long coat. Mrs. Thomas' Endcliffe Muriel is of excellent color and type, as are her smaller Endcliffe Midge and Endcliffe Margery. Her Ch. Endcliffe Merit, who was known in England as Persimmon, has carried off a large share of the show-ring honors. Mrs. Phelan's Mascotte is also worthy of mention as is Mrs. Senn's Queen of the Fairies. These Yorkies represent some of the few really good products of American breeding.

The *American Kennel Gazette* of July 31, 1924, contained an article entitled "Toy Breeds of Today," written by Frank T. Eskrigge. His reference to Yorkies states that New England was for many years the center of Yorkshire enthusiasts in this country. But in later years the entries appear to have shifted from New England to the New York area. Mr. Eskrigge shows a picture of Ch. Rochdale Queenie and states that she is owned by Mr. and Mrs. John

Shipp of Englewood, R. I., and was owned by Emanuel Battersby of New England, one of the earliest fanciers of the breed, until he died. At the time of this article Queenie had recently won Best Toy at a Providence, R. I., show.

Mrs. W. A. Beck of Watsonville, California, established her Niquoia Kennel in 1900; her original stock was the Pellon Yorkie from England. Also in California in the 1920's and 1930's were Irma Copeland, Mrs. Denver Harmon, Henry Beckwith, Mrs. Annie Reid of Seattle, Washington, and Colonel John Rose of Canada. Colonel Rose's most famous Yorkie of this time was his imported Ch. Little Jetsom, who won 19 Best Toy Dog awards and three Best in Show awards. Many of the famous Rose Yorkies bred by the Colonel still appear in pedigrees of California and Canadian Yorkies today.

During this same period, breeders and showers of Yorkies in the East and Midwest included Harry Draper of Toronto, Henry T. Shannon of Carey, Illinois, Mrs. Harriet Riddock of Detroit and Mr. and Mrs. Crosthwaite.

International Ch. Bond's Byngo.

The only so-called International Champions during this time were International Ch. Haslingden Dandy Dinty, imported by Andrew Patterson; International Ch. Bond's Byngo, bred by Harry

Ch. Petit Wee Wee with his breeder-owner, Goldie Stone.

Indie Rice with eleven tiny champions.

Draper and imported by Mrs. Riddock; International Ch. Byngo's Royal Masher, bred by Mrs. Riddock and International Ch. Durgin's Mickey bred by Mrs. Myrtle Durgin.

Another of the oldest breeders in the United States was Mrs. Goldie Stone, who established her kennel in 1929 and founded the first strain of Yorkies in the United States. She purchased her first bitch, May Blossom, from Mrs. Riddock and had her bred to International Ch. Bond's Byngo. From May Blossom, Madam Be You (purchased from Mr. Shannon) and Pellon Lady Azure this strain was founded. From her Petite Kennel Mrs. Stone showed her home-bred Yorkies with great success from 1931 to 1955. She retired from showing and bred very few Yorkies after this time due to the ill health of herself and her husband.

Mrs. Stone bred and showed to their championship 17 Yorkies. Her 18th champion, the famous Ch. Petit Byngo Boy, was purchased from Mrs. Riddock. When Mrs. Stone showed her Yorkies they never failed to place in the groups, and this was a rare thing for Yorkies in those days. Like so many early breeders, Mrs. Stone did not show a dog until it was in full coat or "full bloom," as they used to say.

Her Ch. Petit Wee Wee was shown 20 times, winning Best of Breed 19 times and placing first in the Toy Group 14 times. Ch. Petite Baby Jill, sister of Wee Wee, was also shown 20 times, winning 19 Best of Breeds and placing first in 7 Toy Groups. Her last champion, Ch. Petit Magnificent Prince, won Best of Breed and placed first in the Toy Group at his first show in 1952. In 1954 in Delaware, Ohio, he won Best in Show at an All-Breed Show; he was the first American-bred Yorkie to win this honor. At his last show in Columbus, Ohio, in 1955, he won the Toy Group.

As each champion was retired, Mrs. Stone called in a photographer for a final picture of the dog in his blue and gold mantle. Then she tied a cord close to the dog's body around one swatch of blue coat and one swatch of golden head coat and clipped the swatch off. The entire coat was clipped so the dog could enjoy a comfortable home life, but the swatch was saved. These token samples of each champion's coat were carefully wrapped, marked with the dog's name and saved. Unless you had seen them you could never imagine a more magnificent memento of a breeding and show career. The lengths and colors of the hair are beyond description.

Mrs. Fred Rice of California was a fancier of the breed for

many years before she ever showed one. "Indie," as she is known to her friends, was born in the San Francisco area in 1877. As a teenager she saw her first Yorkie. It was in an open carriage in the arms of a "shady lady" who was often driven around the San Francisco area by her coachman. For Indie, it was instant love for the breed, and her parents searched until they located an old Irishman who had imported a few of them. They bought her first Yorkie for her in 1890, and to this day she has never been without at least one. Kitty-Kitty, a tiny Yorkie purchased from Mrs. Beck, was one of her early ones.

Mrs. Rice owned and showed to their championship many tiny Yorkies during the 1940's and 1950's but bred very few of them. She always said that she was too busy collecting and showing tiny ones to bother breeding them. Her special love was always the tiny ones, so she bought them from people who did breed them and she always kept them groomed to perfection. She appeared many times on television, in magazines, in newspapers and in books with groups of her tiny Yorkies, doing much to popularize the breed in the early forties and fifties. She was always very young in spirit and attended her last dog show in June, 1966 in Los Angeles, where she showed her own entry. She was eighty-nine years old at the time.

Ch. Fritty.

Goldie Stone met Mr. and Mrs. Arthur Mills for the first time in 1936 at the Morris and Essex Show where she was exhibiting. This was apparently when the Mills' became interested in the breed, since in 1938 Mr. Mills went to England looking for Yorkies to show and as basic breeding stock. He brought back seven Yorkies. Four of these original imports appear often in the pedigrees of the Yorkies bred and shown in the United States from 1940 to 1950. These dogs were Ch. Fritty, Ch. Suprema, Millbarry's Nell of Invincia and Dainty Tiny. A fifth, Ch. Miss Wynsum, gained fame in the show ring along with Fritty, Suprema and Ch. Millbarry's Sho Sho, who was Suprema's son. After many shows in the East, Mr. Mills came to California with Ch. Miss Wynsum and Fritty (who was not yet a champion). Mary Carlisle, a movie actress, bought Fritty and soon finished his championship. Miss Carlisle and her mother, Mrs. Leota Wytock, also owned Ch. June Rose, imported from Canada, and Raemon of Soham. Ch. Fritty was shown across the United States and had an illustrious show record.

Mrs. Gwen Krakeur of California bought Ch. Suprema and bitches from Mr. Mills and started a small kennel where she bred many famous West Coast Yorkies. In 1945 she also purchased the already famous Ch. Millbarry's Sho Sho from Mr. Mills. She showed Sho Sho during 1945, 1946 and 1947 and in 1945, when Yorkies placed in only 16 Toy Groups for the year, 11 of these placings were won by Sho Sho.

During this time and until 1953, a large percentage of West Coast Yorkies in the show rings were sired by Sho Sho, Fritty or Suprema and their offspring. Many of Mrs. Rice's tiny champions were from these breedings. These studs, as well as Millbarry bitches, were prominent in the background of Yorkies raised by Mrs. Lilly Harris, Kay Finch, Bette Trudgian, Sally Myers, Ruby Bixler and Nell Fietinghoff. The most famous son of Sho Sho was Ch. Tidbit, bred by Ruby Bixler and shown to his championship by Kay Finch. His name still appears in West Coast pedigrees. Ch. Fritty lived his remaining days with Mrs. Rice after Miss Carlisle married and moved to South America.

On February 21 and 22, 1931, the Catalina Kennel Club held an American Kennel Club approved show at Tucson, Arizona. Sixty-nine dogs of all breeds were entered, with one Yorkie entered in the "Novice Bitch Class." She was Misty, owned by Mrs. M. Leighton and, per the catalog, "listed, particulars not known." Misty won

Mary Carlisle with Fritty and ribbons.

Ch. Sir Michael of Astolat with owner Betty G. Trudgian.

her class and went on to win the Toy Group and Best in Show! It is sad to relate that when the records reached the AKC, the win was cancelled under Dog Show Rules, Section 5, Article 7, which states that only dogs whelped in the United States, Canada, Mexico or Cuba are eligible for the Novice Class. A handwritten notation in the catalog notes that Misty was born in England. The microfilm of Misty's show record gives only the date of this show and the cancellation of the win, giving no further record of her being shown. Possibly she was registered later on under another name and shown again, but there is no record of this. Undoubtedly this would have been the first Best-in-Show win at an All-Breed Show in the United States for a Yorkshire Terrier. (We thank

Goldie Stone for putting us on the track of this rumor and Mr. John Brownell for having the AKC records checked to verify the story.)

With painstaking care Mrs. Stone copied from the AKC *Gazette* records of Yorkies shown in the United States from 1931 through 1952 with their group wins. From these records I have listed all Yorkies with two or more group wins. The name of the owner is listed only with the first reference to the dog.

1932—Yorkies exhibited at 25 shows and placed in 4 Groups. Famous Yorkies this year were Rochdale Queen of the Toys and Rochdale Honey, both owned by John Shipp, and Petite Queen of the Fancy, owned by Goldie Stone.

1933—Exhibited at 27 shows and placed in 15 Groups. Mr. A. Patterson won a Group 4th at Westminster with his Earl Byng; Rochdale Queen of the Toys placed in 3 Groups; George Roberts was in 3 Groups with his Harrogate Blue Bell and Harrogate Ladybug; Mrs. Riddock was in 2 Groups with Ch. Byngo's Royal Masher.

1934—Exhibited at 49 shows and placed in 21 Groups. Andrew Patterson won a Group 3rd with Ch. Haslingden Dandy Dinty at Westminster; Acushla, owned and bred by R. A. Crosthwaite, placed in 5 Groups; Ch. Byngo's Royal Masher in 4 Groups; Goldie Stone's Petites in 3 Groups; J. Shipps' Rochdales in 2 Groups.

1935—Exhibited at 36 shows and placed in 10 Groups. Ch. Rochdale Queen of the Toys won a Group 3rd at Westminster and placed in one other Group; Goldie Stone's Petites placed in 3 Groups and Ch. Byngo's Royal Masher in 2 Groups.

1936—Exhibited at 36 shows and placed in 22 Groups. Bobby B. III, owned by Samuel Baxter, won a Group 3rd at Westminster; Petit Wee Wee won 4 Group 1sts for Goldie Stone; Ch. Byngo's Royal Tiny placed in 3 Groups for Mrs. L. Turnbull; Ch. Byngo's Royal Masher had 2 Group placings as did Ch. Achushla.

1937—Exhibited at 54 shows and placed in the Group 19 times. Bobby B. III again won Group 3rd at Westminster; Goldie Stone's Petites placed in the Groups 5 times with 2 1sts; Ch. Acushla placed in 2 Groups.

1938—Exhibited at 51 shows with 30 Group placings. Goldie Stone's Petites won 9 Group 1sts with Ch. Petit Wee Wee winning 7 of them; Miss Wynsum owned by Arthur Mills, won 4 Group

1sts; Lawlock's Little Tootie placed in the Group 5 times and
Feather of Castlethorpe, owned by the late Blanche Dunbar,
placed in 2 Groups.

1939—Exhibited at 58 shows and placed in 37 Groups. Ch. Petite
Baby Jill won 7 Group 1sts and Petit Lord Dandy II won 2
Group 1sts for Goldie Stone; Ch. Miss Wynsum won 4 Group
1sts and placed 6 more times in the group for Arthur Mills; Ch.
Fritty placed in 7 Groups with 4 of them 1sts; Alexandrine of
Soham, owned by Mrs. C. F. Dowe, placed in 3 Groups.

1940—Exhibited at 63 shows and placed in 33 Groups. Alexandrine
of Soham placed in 6 Groups with one 1st; Harris, owned by
Mrs. P. A. Johnson, placed in 4 Groups; Ch. Fritty placed in 5
Groups with 3 1sts while Raemon of Soham placed in 3 Groups
with 2 1sts; Blue Boy of Dorn placed in 3 Groups with one 1st.

1941—Exhibited at 73 shows and placed in 32 Groups. Ch. Fritty
placed in 5 Groups with 2 1sts; Ch. Harris placed in 5 Groups;
Ch. Alexandrine of Soham placed in 4 Groups; Ch. Blue Knight,
owned by Mrs. E. A. Smith, placed in 4 Groups with one 1st;
Ch. Petit Wee placed in 3 Groups with one 1st; Harringay
High Tracy won 3 Group placings for Mrs. M. F. Wagner;
Henderson's Pretty Girl won 2 Group placings for Mrs. A. Hen-
derson.

1942—Exhibited at 56 shows and placed in 29 Groups. Ch. Olinda
Pearl, owned by Mrs. E. A. Smith, placed in 7 Groups with one
1st; Ch. Suprema, imported by Arthur Mills and owned then
by Mrs. G. H. Krakeur, placed in 5 Groups with 2 1sts; Petites
in 5 Groups with 2 1sts; Ch. Alexandrine of Soham in 3 Groups
with one 1st; Durgin's Mickey, owned by Myrtle Durgin, placed
in 2 Groups; Millbarry's Duchess, owned by Arthur Mills, placed
in 3 Groups.

1943—Exhibited at 33 shows and placed in 11 Groups. Ch. Alex-
andrine of Soham placed in 2 Groups as did Millbarry's Sho
Sho, with one 1st for Sho Sho, who was then owned by Vera
Zorina.

1944—Exhibited at 42 shows and placed in 24 Groups. Westminster
1st in the Toy Group was won by Millbarry's Sho Sho, who
also won 3 other Group placings; Ch. Durgin's Mickey placed
in 4 groups; Ch. Olinda Pearl placed in 2 Groups as did Petite
Wisp of Silk, owned by Goldie Stone; Wisp of Silk had one
Group 1st.

1945—Exhibited at 28 shows and placed in 16 Groups. Ch. Mill-

barry's Sho Sho, now owned by Mrs. Krakeur, won 8 Group
1sts and 3 Group placings, taking 11 Group placings out of 16
for all Yorkies that year. Ch. Durgin's Mickey placed in 2
Groups.

1946—Exhibited at 55 shows and placed in 29 Groups. Ch. Durgin's
Mickey placed in 8 Groups and won 2 1sts; Ch. Little Boy Blue
of Yorktown, owned by Mrs. R. Bedford, placed in 8 Groups;
Ch. Millbarry's Sho Sho placed in 6 Groups with 2 1sts; For-
ever Amber of Crowncrest, owned by Mrs. Fred Rice, placed
in 2 Groups.

1947—Exhibited at 58 shows with 22 Group placings. Ch. Pretty
Please, owned by Kay Finch, placed in 7 Groups with one 1st;
Ch. Durgin's Mickey placed in 2 Groups as did Frittalaria,
owned by I. E. Copeland.

1948—Exhibited at 60 shows and placed in 31 Groups. Ch. Gwen-
mar's Bitty Britches, owned by Mrs. Fred Rice, had 2 1sts and
4 other Group placings; Ch. Pretty Please placed in 6 Groups;
Ch. Little Boy Blue of Yorktown placed in 5 Groups with one
1st; Ch. Durgin's Mickey placed in 3 Groups.

1949—Exhibited at 87 shows and placed in 21 Groups. Ch. Gwen-
mar's Bitty Britches placed in 3 Groups; Vaki, owned by Mrs.
V. P. Anderson, placed in 3 Groups; Ch. Petit Wee Billy Boy,
owned by Ruby Ericksen, placed in 2 Groups; Bitsy Budget of
Crowncrest, owned by Kay Finch, placed in 2 Groups; Burlin-
game Top Hat, owned by R. Layte, also placed in 2 Groups
with one 1st.

1950—Exhibited at 109 shows and placed in 27 Groups. Haslingden
Wee Girlie, owned by Mrs. C. Heim, placed in 3 Groups; Hi-
falutin, owned by Pearl Johnson, placed in 3 Groups; Ch. Durgin's Pilot placed in 3 Groups with one 1st for Myrtle Durgin;
Little Sir Model, owned by Mrs. Joan Gordon, won 2 Group
1sts; Blue Dolly, also owned by Mrs. Gordon, had 2 Group
placings with one 1st; Holly of Achmonie, owned by Mrs. Ferguson, 2 group placings; Durgin's Beatrice, 2 Group placings
with one 1st for her owner, Mrs. S. Quick; Tidbit, owned by
Kay Finch, 2 placings with one 1st.

1951—Exhibited at 116 shows with 44 Group placings. Ch. Little
Sir Model placed in 12 Groups, 8 of them Group 1sts, and went
on to win 3 Best in Show at All-Breed Dog Shows. Durgin's
Lady Dorothy placed in 4 Groups with two 1sts for Mrs. Town-
send; Ch. Durgin's Pilot placed in 2 Groups, both 1sts; Ch.

Ch. Tidbit (Charlie), famous California dog and group winner. (Ruby Bixler, breeder.)

Pixie Prince of Crowncrest, 4 Group placings with one 1st for Mrs. Fred Rice; Clu Mor Nina, 4 Group placings with one 1st for Mrs. Ferguson.

1952—Exhibited at 124 shows with 67 Group placings. Ch. Little Sir Model placed in 27 Groups, winning 13 1sts and one Best in Show at an All-Breed Dog Show for the Gordon-Bennett sisters; Ch. Clu Mor Nina, 4 Group placings with 3 1sts; Ch. Fantasy of Crowncrest, 5 Group placings with one 1st for Bette Trudgian; Ch. Pixie Prince of Crowncrest, 4 Group placings; Petite Magnificent Prince, 3 Group placings and two of them 1sts for Goldie Stone; Pride of Leyton, owned by Catherine Miller, 4 Group placings with one 1st; Ch. Petite Souvenir, owned by Ruby Ericksen, 3 Group placings; Ch. Star Twilight of Clu Mor, owned by Joan Gordon and Janet Bennett, 2 Group placings with one 1st.

From these years of show records you can see how the breed was increasing in popularity. To bring any breed to success and prominence, people with the interests of the breed at heart are needed. All can be interested in different phases of the breed, but they come together with each one doing his part. Some are breeders, some fanciers and some merely interested in showing and training dogs, but each person is needed.

In 1950 Kay Finch of California and Bette Trudgian started working together to organize the Yorkshire Terrier Club of America. Both of these ladies are now prominent American Kennel Club Judges. Kay Finch became much more famous for her Afghan kennel a few years later, but she has never lost her love for the Yorkies.

Kay Finch, center, showing Petit Point in 1951.

The club was formed in 1951. Kay was the first president and Bette was the first secretary. Prominent on this list were members who were active in the club. They were: Captain and Mrs. C. H. Anderson, Janet E. Bennett, Grace Benoist, Alpha Collins, Harry Draper, Blanche Dunbar, Paul and Myrtle Durgin, LeMoyne Eastwood, Ruby Ericksen, Ethyl Ferguson, Braden and Kay Finch, Joan Gordon, Lily Harris, Pearl Johnson (Kinkarte), Violet and Ruth Kahn, Mary J. K. Mills, Sally Myers, Susan Pike, Indie Rice, Aileen Rusco (Martello), Ethel Schrader, Goldie Stone, Iola Suhr (Dowd), Ronald Thompson, Theron and Bette Trudgian, Myrtle Watts and William Wynne. Altogether there were 68 charter members.

The Yorkshire Terrier Club of America held its first AKC-sanctioned match in 1954 and its first Specialty Show in 1955. It was accepted as a member club of the American Kennel Club in 1958. From the forming of the club, records were kept and many articles were published about the prominent Yorkies and their breeders. There are so many prominent Yorkies and breeders today and so many good dogs that space does not permit me to list all of them.

Many people still ask about Corporal Smoky. She is part of the history of Yorkies in America, and we were fortunate to contact her owner to confirm some facts and correct misinformation that had been written about her. Her owner, William Wynne, was a charter member of the club. He is now a roving reporter and photographer for the *Cleveland Plain Dealer*. Here is Smoky's story.

Smoky was the most decorated and best-known American-owned dog in the Pacific and Asiatic areas during World War II. She was found by Edward Downey of Norristown, Pennsylvania, in February of 1944 in an abandoned Japanese foxhole in the jungle near Nadzab, New Guinea. When found, Smoky weighed less than four pounds and was thought to be about one year old. She understood neither English nor Japanese, so her original owners may have been Dutch or Javanese, but no one ever found out where she had come from.

Downey gave her to Corporal Dare, who thought her long coat was too hot for her, so he cut off her hair. Dare was a poker player, and in a game where he was losing he offered to sell Smoky to Corporal Wynne for two Australian pounds ($6.22 in American money at that time). Wynne bought Smoky and Dare returned to his game.

It took Wynne from March to August of 1944 to discover that Smoky was a Yorkshire Terrier. This identification was made with the help of the July issue of *National Geographic Magazine,* in which there were color plates and stories about Yorkies.

Wynne was then with a photo reconnaisance squadron of the Air Force, and Smoky became a squadron member. Wynne was an excellent teacher and trainer and Smoky was an exceptionally bright pupil, and she soon learned many tricks and entertained hundreds of servicemen in hospitals in Australia, New Guinea and the Phillipines during her two years of active service in the Air Force. Her blanket was made of green felt from a card table and was covered with her many decorations and medals. In addition to her corporal's stripes, she wore the Fifth Air Force badge, the 26th Photo Insignia, the Air Wings, a Photo Technician badge, a Red Cross badge and, last but not least, a WAC badge. After all, Smoky was a lady! All of these honors were in addition to her Theatre of Operations Ribbons.

Her tricks consisted of tightrope walking, praying, waltzing, playing dead, running and jumping through hoops and spelling her

Corporal Smoky. She was the most famous and most decorated American-owned mascot in the Pacific and Asiatic areas during World War II.

own name. She did this regardless of how the letters were mixed. Aside from her entertaining, she was called into active duty with the signal corps. With a bit of persuasion, Smoky pulled a telegraph wire through an 8-inch pipe for a distance of 70 feet under an air strip. She saved the signal corps many man-hours of digging.

During her active service Smoky went through a typhoon on Okinawa, from which a slight cold was the only aftermath. She was in 150 air raids on New Guinea, with a few shivers of fright, and 13 air-sea rescue missions without being airsick. She also made numerous parachute jumps from a thirty-foot tower in her own chute, which was made from money belts given to her by her many admirers. *Yank Magazine* gave her the title of "Champion Mascot of the Southwest Pacific."

After their retirement from the service, Smoky and her master appeared on the stage and at boxing arenas and traveled all over the United States with a circus. They performed through various media to an estimated 6 million people. In 1950 they were on television for 42 weeks in Cleveland, Ohio, and during this time Smoky never repeated a trick. They retired again, but in 1954 Wynne took Smoky out of retirement for their own thirty-week show on television. The program was called "How to Train Your Dog."

Smoky was buried on January 21, 1957, after a very active, adventurous life. Very few dogs have ever exceeded her in bravery or intelligence, regardless of their breeding or size.

In our last tribute to this wonderful little Yorkie, we still wonder where she came from, who her original owner was and what her background was. None of this is necessary though, since she made her own place in life.

CHAPTER 4

American Breeders and Fanciers—1950 to 1970

Since the formation of the Yorkshire Terrier Club of America, the popularity of the breed has increased each year. In England also the popularity increased during this time, until Yorkies are among the top breeds that they export today. Each year more Yorkies appear in shows in England and on the Continent, as well as in America, and it is a rare thing to attend a show today where there is no Yorkie entry.

As popularity of the breed increased, more names of people who bred and showed them came into prominence. I regret that it is impossible to show pictures of the many wonderful Yorkies of today or even to list all of their breeders, but these are easily located in the show rings and in current dog magazines. Here are some of the more prominent names, listed by geographical areas of the United States.

In the early days in the East were: Mildred Hornbrook, who

English, American and Canadian Ch. Progress of Progresso. (Bud Priser and Jim Nickerson, owners.) He distinguished himself by going Best in Show in all three countries.

The late Mr. Leo C. Wilson, editor of English Dog World *and judge, shown with author. Photo by Cooke and Son.*

started many present-day breeders with her carefully selected stock; Jud and Lucia Houston; David and Nancy Lerner; Maybelle Neuguth (now deceased); Rita Patterson; Frances Corkhill and Myrtle Young. Later came Kathleen Dollman; Lucy Duffy; Mrs. C. Groverman Ellis; Vivian Horney; Morris Howard; Johnny Robinson; Beryl Hesketh; Merrill Cohen and Betty Dullinger. Mr. Cohen and Mrs. Dullinger are now AKC judges. During the past six years Ann Seranne and Barbara Wolferman have attained prominence in the show ring and as breeders. By planned breeding and selection, they in turn have started many of the new breeders in their area.

In the Southeast and South were: Felix and Winifred Drake and Bettie Wooten. Later came Barbara Francis and Harriet Karns.

In the Midwest older breeders and fanciers were: Mary Jane Davis; Shirley Marble; Helen Modic and the Neumanns. Following them were Jim Nickerson and Bud Priser; Ray Ryan and Ken Thompson; Lynn Devan; Mary Sapovchak; Pauline Miller; Betty Nunley and Hazel Thrasher. Still later were: Dr. Charles Chap-

Barbara Wolferman holding Ch. Mayfair's Oddfella and his four-month-old son.

Ch. Mayfair's Tiddlewinks. He weighed in at 3½ lbs.

man; Val Kilkeary and Judy Tyma; Barbara Bartels; Royce Baldwin; Virginia Knoche; Grace Shackelford; Kay Radcliffe; Jim Brunkhorst and Pearl Trojan. Mrs. L. S. Gordon, Jr. and Miss Janet Bennett have been the most prominent exhibitors and breeders for many years and have started many of the present-day breeders in Yorkies.

In the West, Ron Thompson of Canada started showing and breeding Yorkies when he was fourteen years old. From that time until today he has shown and/or bred the top Yorkies in Canada. Many of his Yorkies are also American champions.

The Northwest had: Ila Clark; Betty Donahoo; Melba Green; Frances Hickman and Margaret Van Hulten. Later came Carol Foster; Lorna Jordan and Vivian Foster.

In Southern California were: Stella Davis; Ruth Fields; Nell Fietinghoff; the Ross Gasts; the Gowings; the Hornungs; Pearl Kincarte; Muriel Krieg and Lee and Mary Schaller. Nell Fietinghoff, Ruth Fields and Muriel Krieg were officers of the Yorkshire Terrier Club for many years, and Muriel Krieg was also the founder and first editor of the club newsletter. Pearl Kincarte obedience-trained many tiny Yorkies and showed them at hospitals, parades and

Ch. Raybrook's Rear Admiral. (Ray Ryan and Ken Thompson, breeders.)

Ann Seranne holding Ch. Topsy of Tolestar.

convalescent homes. Mrs. Kincarte devoted many years to this charitable project.

Newer breeders in the California area are: Lorraine Berry; Anne Goldman; Edyce Keniston and Wendy Whiteley. Mrs. Whiteley is also an AKC judge.

CHAPTER 5

The Revised Standard for the Breed

From the time the first Yorkies were shown in America and accepted as a breed by the American Kennel Club, they were judged by the standard of the Yorkshire Terrier Club of England. This is the first revision of the standard ever made in America; it was revised by the Yorkshire Terrier Club of America, Inc. and approved by the American Kennel Club in May, 1966.

THE STANDARD OF THE YORKSHIRE TERRIER

GENERAL APPEARANCE—That of a long-haired Toy Terrier whose blue and tan coat is parted on the face and from the base of the skull to the end of the tail and hangs evenly and quite straight down each side of body. The body is neat, compact and well proportioned. The dog's high-head carriage and confident manner should give the appearance of vigor and self-importance.

HEAD—Small and rather flat on top, the skull not too prominent or round, the muzzle not too long, with the bite neither undershot nor overshot and teeth sound. Either scissor or level bite is acceptable. The nose is black. Eyes are medium in size and not too prominent: dark in color and sparkling with a sharp, intelligent expression. Eye rims are dark. Ears are small V-shaped, carried erect and set not too far apart.

BODY—Well proportioned and very compact. The back is rather short, the back line level, with height at shoulder the same as at the rump.

LEGS AND FEET—Forelegs should be straight, elbows neither in nor out. Hind legs straight when viewed from behind, but stifles are moderately bent when viewed from the sides. Feet are round with black toenails. Dew claws, if any, are generally removed from the hind legs. Dew claws on the forelegs may be removed.

TAIL—Docked to a medium length and carried slightly higher than the level of the back.

COAT—Quality, texture and quantity of coat are of prime importance. Hair is glossy, fine and silky in texture. Coat on the body is moderately long and perfectly straight (not wavy). It may be trimmed to floor length to give ease of movement and a neater appearance, if desired. The fall on the head is long, tied with one bow in center of head or parted in the middle and tied with two bows. Hair on muzzle is very long. Hair should be trimmed short on tips of ears and may be trimmed on feet to give them a neat appearance.

COLORS—Puppies are born black and tan and are normally darker in body color, showing an intermingling of black hair in the tan until they are matured. Color of hair on body and richness of tan on head and legs are of prime importance in adult dogs, to which the following color requirements apply:

> BLUE: Is a dark steel-blue, not a silver-blue and not mingled with fawn, bronze or black hairs.

> TAN: All tan hair is darker at the roots than in the middle, shading to still lighter tan at the tips. There should be no sooty or black hair intermingled with any of the tan.

> COLOR ON BODY: The blue extends over the body from back of neck to root of tail. Hair on tail is a darker blue, especially at end of tail.

> HEADFALL: A rich, golden tan, deeper in color at sides of head, at ear roots and on the muzzle, with ears a deep, rich tan. Tan color should not extend down on back of neck.

> CHEST AND LEGS: A bright, rich tan, not extending above the stifle on the hind legs.

WEIGHT—Must not exceed seven pounds.

Please note that the old point system, which followed the standard, has been deleted by the AKC. I feel that this was a good thing for the breed, since too many points were quoted for color, quality and quantity of coat. These things are important,

Semi-erect

Too Large

CORRECT

Flop or Drop Ear

Wide-set

Correct and incorrect ear carriage and placement.

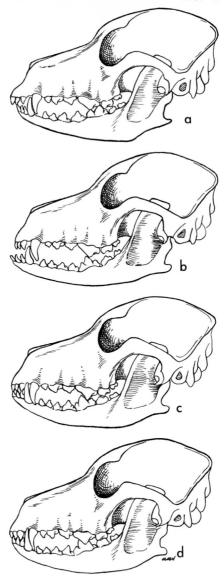

Correct and incorrect mouths and jaws.

a. OVERSHOT— the upper jaw protrudes over the lower jaw.
b. UNDERSHOT— the lower jaw protrudes beyond the upper jaw.
c. LEVEL BITE— upper and lower teeth meet.
d. SCISSOR BITE— teeth come together as blades in a pair of scissors.

*A and B both are bad mouths. C and D are considered the only correct
bites in America, but in England and on the Continent D is considered the
only correct bite for breeding and showing.*

*Teeth are 42 in number, with 12 incisors or front teeth (6 upper and 6
lower), 4 canine or eye teeth and 26 molars (12 upper and 14 lower).*

but nothing is more important than a good, solid body with a straight back and sound legs to hold up the dog and this coat. A good coat can usually be grown with care, effort and brushing, but nothing will correct an unsound body.

Head—The skull should not be too domed or round on top. There should be no open fontanelle or soft spot on head, since this should close before dog matures. Eyes should not protrude as do those of a Pekingese, but should be of medium size, dark and not too round. (Plate two and Plate three show correct and incorrect mouths and ear sets.)

Body—The body should not be long, thin and stringy. The back should be straight, not high in the rear or at the shoulders, nor should it be roached. (Plate four)

Legs and Feet—Watch for hip joints that pop out of the socket and make the dog lame. Stifles should not have loose, sloppy muscles, permitting the joints to slip in and out of the sockets. Neither front nor hind legs should bow out or in at the joints but should be solid and firm. Keep excess hair from between pads so the foot is comfortable, and cut excess hair to make the foot look round.

Tail—The tail should be carried slightly higher than the level of the back, with a long plume on the end which floats gracefully behind the dog as he walks. A tail set too low on the spine makes the body look long and humped. A tail too straight up or bending toward the dog's head spoils the general appearance.

Coat—On a mature Yorkie coat should be fine, silky, thick and glossy. Should also hang straight without any sign of wave or curl. Should never be kinky or fuzzy on the hindquarters. If the coat is so profuse that the dog cannot walk easily with an unwrapped coat, don't be afraid to trim the ends off evenly to floor length. This improves the movement of the dog without detracting from the beauty of the coat.

Colors: Blue—The blue of the body coat is not platinum, light silver-blue or black on a mature Yorkie. The dark steel-blue is like the color you find on an old sharp-edged steel cutting knife when it is cleaned and polished. The steel-blue of a gun barrel is sometimes referred to as the proper color, but most breeders feel that this color is too nearly black. Published records show that the description of the color as "blue" has always been a point of controversy. Here are the names of the books, dates of publication and the references pertaining to "blue."

Roach back

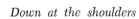

Down at the shoulders

Correct back

Correct and incorrect back lines.

Tail set too low

Tail too gay

CORRECT tail set

ARH

Correct and incorrect tail carriage.

Dr. Gordon Stables' book, published about 1884, states, "Colour silver-blue on the back . . ."

Robert Leighton's book, published in 1907, states, "Colour dark steel-blue. . . ." He also gives the Standard for the Paisley or Clydesdale Terrier, from which most old-timers feel the original standard for the Yorkie was copied, since the two standards are almost identical. For color this standard reads, "A level, bright steel-blue, extend from the back of the neck to the root of the tail. The head, legs and feet should be a clear, bright, golden tan, free from grey, sooty or black hairs." Doesn't this sound familiar?

James Watson's book, published in 1916, states that the first standard used for judging in England reads, "Colour—a bright steel-blue. . . ."

Lillian Mallock, in her book *All Toy Breeds*, published in the early 1900's, says that she has had Yorkies in her family for over forty years. Her description of the body coat reads, "Bright steel-blue and in no account mingled with fawn or dark hairs."

Jessop describes body coat as, "Bright steel-blue," so evidently this was in the original edition. In one of his revised editions his standard reads, "A dark steel-blue (not silver-blue)."

From these many different opinions I draw the conclusion that if the original standard for the breed was copied from the standard of the Clydesdale or Paisley, as it appears to have been, the original standard did read "bright steel-blue." So if the standard was rewritten in those early days there is no record of it, but you will note that not one authority ever said that the body coat was black.

Most of these older writers had the feeling that the lighter blue and the dark blue were both necessary in breeding to obtain the proper shade of blue. Otherwise in breeding light males to light females you would end up with grey bodies and cream-colored heads, and breeding Yorkies which were too black you would get dogs with orange heads and black bodies.

© Holt

CHAPTER 6

Selecting Your Yorkie

Know what you want when you plan to buy your first Yorkie. You may have in mind a pet, a bitch for breeding, a dog for stud or a show-quality Yorkie. Read everything about the breed that you can find. See as many Yorkies in shows and in pictures as you can. By studying these dogs, pictures and the breed standard you will soon recognize good qualities, faults and points that you do not care for. Accept the fact that all dogs have at least one fault and recognize it as such. Never try to convince yourself that faults do not exist in *any* dog simply because you want to buy the dog or because you like it. In facing the fact that you have a dog with a fault or are going to buy one, you are on your way to becoming a good breeder or a good fancier of the breed. When you admit and recognize a fault you can start to eliminate and correct it by linebreeding.

Once you buy your stock, it costs no more to raise a litter of good puppies than it does to raise a litter of poor puppies. The good ones are easier to sell because you know they are good and they show that they are good.

For the novice, a pet quality puppy is the wisest investment. You learn about the breed from him as he grows, and this will help you select better breeding stock in the future. Never feel that you are buying an inferior puppy simply because you buy him at pet price. He will be just as intelligent, make just as good a pet and often is just as handsome as his more expensive litter mates. Ethical breeders are interested in improving their breeding, and they grade their litters and sell as pets puppies who have a fault the breeder feels could be passed on to the progeny of this puppy— or he may only have a small fault that keeps him from being shown.

In larger breeds females are spayed and males are castrated before they are sold as pets, but this is seldom done in toy breeds since there is too much danger to the puppy's life. If these pet-priced puppies are neither castrated nor spayed, the breeder must protect his bloodlines by placing them where they will not be bred. Generally the breeder draws up a contract in duplicate describing

Davedwil Iney's Petite Spice, the pivot around which the author's breeding program has been planned.

the dog, giving his registration number if he has one and stating that the dog is being sold as a pet for the improvement of the breed and is not to be bred. He may even state what the dog's fault is. Both copies are dated and signed by both the seller and the buyer with each party getting a copy. The reason for this is that the original buyer may be completely honest and plan to abide by the seller's wishes but for some reason the dog could go to another party who would want to breed it. In such a case the breeder can send a photostat of his agreement to the American Kennel Club

Three of the author's dogs: Little Topper of Lilactime, with sons.

explaining why the dog was not to be bred, and they will respect his rights for trying to improve the breed. Therefore the offspring of that puppy would not be registered.

Never feel badly about buying a puppy under these circumstances, because you know that you are buying him from someone who loves him, wants him to have the best home possible and yet must protect the breed and his business investment. Only honest and knowledgeable breeders sell pets in this manner. The dishonest breeder or one who knows no better registers all puppies, thinks they are all fit for breeding and usually charges much more for inferior puppies or deliberately covers up a fault and sells it as a perfect specimen.

If you feel you want to start with breeding stock, your best buy is a good bitch puppy from good bloodlines who can be bred back into her own lines. Most breeders are careful where they sell these brood-sized puppies, since they are the most valuable puppies that they raise. A good bitch puppy, sound of body and limb and with good ancestry, is an invaluable foundation for any future breeding program or starting your own strain. You should have to pay more for this puppy than you would for a tiny bitch who is too small to breed. Your future brood should mature to over five pounds if she is to be strictly a matron, but she should come from lines where the ancestors are not all large and oversized.

If you manage to get a nice strong bitch who matures to seven pounds you are lucky, and don't let anyone tell you that she is too big to produce small puppies. This all depends on what ancestors she has and how you breed her. Also, they may tell you that they have bred a three-pound bitch. Maybe they did, but if the three-pound bitch whelped normally without complications and delivered strong, healthy puppies, she was the exception to the rule. Most of these tiny bitches must have Caesarians to deliver their puppies if they are lucky enough to carry them until delivery time. Many cannot even carry the puppies full-time and often die from complications of carrying them or from the Caesarian to deliver them. They seldom deliver sound, strong puppies. Also, the mortality rate of these puppies is very high.

When buying breeding stock or show quality stock, you should buy from a reputable, knowledgeable breeder. He will know how to help you with problems as they arise, since he knows his stock. Also, he has a kennel and will probably have several puppies for you to select from. If not, he can advise you when he does have the stock that you want. Usually these breeders have studs that you may use when your bitch puppy is ready to be bred. Always make arrangements in writing regarding future stud services so there will be no misunderstanding later on.

When you locate the breeder who has the stock that you want,

Topper and his photo with his owner, author Aileen Martello. Topper weighed 2 lbs. when full grown.

Incy's Petite Yvonne

tell him exactly what you want—whether it is a pet, breeding stock or a show dog. Don't try to buy something cheap and misrepresent what your plans are, because while an ethical breeder will lose interest in you, an unethical breeder or a novice will be glad to cut price for you. Cheap breeding stock is a very poor investment.

If your choice is a dog for stud, be sure that you don't buy him too young, before he has two testicles in his scrotum. Some males develop at an early age but most of them do not complete development of testicles in view until they are six or seven months old. If testicles are not in the scrotum by that age, they may never develop. Extremely tiny males are not completely developed until later than six or seven months, but even these show the testicles at that age, although they are small.

You should pay more for show quality males or females since the breeder must keep them longer really to know how they are going to develop. A beautiful puppy at three months may turn into an unworthy specimen by the time he is nine or ten months old. Most changes in body structure take place between five and seven months; when the teeth come in and the mouth takes on its permanent shape, the body seems to take on most of its growth change. A Yorkie can stop growing at that age or he can continue to grow until he is eighteen months old. These things you must think about before you fall in love with a young puppy. Also, if you are able to see and know about his ancestors, you will know more about the changes he will be expected to make as he grows.

Read pedigrees from the lines that you choose, see ancestors and study all dogs from this kennel that you can see. Make notes on these dogs and keep them for future reference when you start to breed. Study books on genetics; although this is a technical study, you can learn much about breeding that you need to know.

The one simple fact that genetics teaches you is that like does not produce like, *as such*. This means that you can't look at a male and female that you are planning to mate and know that they will produce puppies who look like either or both of them. A mating merely brings together a collection of sets of genes in a female with the collection of genes in the male. When these genes combine in a mating, they make dominant either the good qualities or the faults of one or both parents. What happens in the puppies depends on which genes are dominant and which are recessive in this *particular* mating. Mated to another

Iney's Petit Mister Tuffett (2¼ pounds).

Mr. Feathers, a 1½ lb. Martello Yorkie shown with his portrait.

dog, the combination would never be quite the same. Linebred dogs are closely related, so continuing to linebreed brings good qualities and faults out into the open in a hurry. When the fault is visible in puppies, you can change bitch or stud in the same lines and try again. This is the only way that you can have a breeding program with any thought of improving the breed. It can't be done by hit-or-miss breeding with any dog who comes along. A good sound bitch who is no beauty but who is properly bred with a good related stud should produce better puppies than she is. If you don't get them, try another stud in her line.

The word *champion* in a pedigree does not mean that this stud or bitch will produce good puppies or even that the dog can produce at all. The misconception of the word *champion* has probably caused more breeding problems, in all breeds, than any other factor. People always feel that if a dog is good enough to earn his championship when he is shown, he *must* produce good puppies. There is no logical reason that he should, unless he is bred with a good, compatible bitch whose genes complement his.

In studying old pedigrees you come across a few studs who are called "prepotent sires." These dogs have been used repeatedly in forming a new breed or improving an old one, and they occur in all breeds. They are studs who passed on more of their good qualities than their faults, and to most bitches, either inside or outside their own lines. These studs are few and far between.

Another thing that you should know before you buy your Yorkie is how to read a pedigree. Ask any experienced breeder to explain this to you, because many breeders buy up litter lots of puppies before they are registered and then register them using their own kennel names. The puppy may be from a completely unrelated bitch bred to one of their studs, or it may not be from their lines at all.

CHAPTER 7

Mating the Yorkshire Terrier

A Yorkie should be fully developed before it is bred. Not only is it cruel to breed a bitch puppy at her first season at the age of six or seven months, but seldom does more than one puppy result. This puppy may be malformed or too weak to live, and with the problems that a little bitch develops from such an early mating she may be ruined as a future brood bitch.

A bitch is considered mature when she has her second season. This usually occurs from one year to eighteen months. If you see no visible signs of season until she is fourteen or fifteen months old, you may assume that this is her second season and that her first season was so slight that it went unnoticed. It is safe to breed her at this age.

Even though you plan on breeding a bitch only one time she should weigh at least 4½ to 5 pounds. But if you are planning to use her in a regular breeding program, she should weigh 6 or 7 pounds.

When a male develops physically at an early age you can use him one time at stud when he is ten or eleven months old if he is very eager. This gives him experience as a stud and makes him easy to handle later on. After this first mating, do not use him again until he is at least eighteen months old. If he is not completely developed or interested in mating when he is under a year old, do not try to force him, since this could ruin him for future stud work. Many males are not ready to be used until they are nearly two years old, so let them take their time and do not be upset if they are late starters.

A young, inexperienced male will play around with a bitch at season without making any actual effort to mate her, but when he is fully developed both mentally and physically the playful attitude will be completely gone.

It is easier to mate a virgin bitch with a proven stud because the virgin bitch is often excitable and hard to control during the first mating. This will frighten a novice male, but her actions

Male reproductive system.

1— *Anus*
2— *Opening of Anal Sac*
3— *Uretha*
4— *Prostate*
5— *Scrotum*
6— *Testicle*
7— *Glans Penis*
8— *Bladder*
9— *Deferent Ducts*
10— *Anal Glands*

Female reproductive system.

1— *Postcava*
2— *Aorta*
3— *Kidney*
4— *Anus*
5— *Neck of Uterus*
6— *Vulva*
7— *Bladder*
8— *Uterus (R. and L. Horns)*
9— *Ovaries*

will not upset a proven stud. Mate a novice male with a proven bitch, as she will be quiet and help him with the mating.

From his first mating, train your stud to expect your help. Put your hands on him and the bitch at different places during his first mating. Then he will never be frightened by hands when you have to help him with a difficult mating. A frightened stud is not a good stud and often strange bitches are temperamental, so you save yourself trouble if you have a cooperative stud.

No one can tell you exactly when a bitch is ready to be bred. During her first few days of season there is little visible evidence because most bitches keep themselves clean. Naturally, they do not bleed as profusely as bitches in larger breeds do. When you expect your bitch in season, put a white towel or cloth in her bed so you will see the first signs. Her vulva start to swell noticeably. After five or six days of bloody discharge the color fades and there is a thick, yellowish discharge. This should be the time to breed her. The eleventh and thirteenth days are considered the best times to breed a Yorkie but all bitches vary, so the best thing to do is to watch her carefully. When she is ready, she will turn her tail from side to side if she is near a male dog. When no male is available for the test, tickle her gently on one of her hind legs near the tail. If she is ready to breed she will turn her tail.

You can also have your veterinarian take a vaginal smear to see if she is at peak season. This is important if you must make a trip or ship the bitch, and it is the most certain way to tell.

If your bitch goes to a stud to be bred, the owner of the stud will know how to handle the mating. Just be sure that she gets there early enough in her season. If you have a male and female and are breeding them for the first time by yourself, you should know how to help them in every possible way.

Plan the mating in a quiet room away from the noise of other dogs. A small, confined area like a bathroom or laundry room is best, for there is less room for the dogs to run around and you will have running water close by. Wash the genitals of both dogs with a washcloth and warm, soapy water before starting the mating. Rinse with clear water and dry them of excess moisture. Use blunt-nosed scissors to trim long hairs carefully from the male's penis and from around the vulva of the bitch. Long hair from either dog can become wrapped around the male's penis during the mating, and if the hair is tightly wrapped and is unnoticed it will go back under the sheath of skin when the penis is retracted. This can stop circulation, cause the penis to rot with infection and may require amputation. This seldom happens, but if you know about the danger it will never happen. Any long-haired dog is subject to this problem.

Have clean towels, small, washable rugs, vaseline and sterilized cotton at hand before you start the mating. If needed, put a small amount of vaseline on a piece of cotton and apply the vaseline just inside the bitch's vulva. Do not insert deeply, and be sure that your hands and fingers are sanitary to avoid any infection as you dilate her vulva.

When the stud is smaller than the bitch, fold rugs for him to stand on to bring him into proper range. If the bitch is smaller, put the rugs under her and stand the stud on the floor. Always give them a rug or some sort of firm footing. The bitch will usually move around to aid the stud. Sit on the floor with the bitch facing you and between your knees. If she is nervous or temperamental you can use your knees to support and control her. Also, your legs are handy for one or the other of the dogs to lean against when they are tied in the mating.

Place one hand underneath the bitch with you first and second fingers on each side of her vulva. Your fingers make a V-shaped support, and this way you can feel how you should move her to aid the entry of the male without disturbing either dog. You can also tell if he is striking her too high or too low and arrange rugs to correct the situation. With your hands in this position you know when he has entered her and is tied to her.

When the tie occurs hold her firmly, especially if she is a virgin or a nervous bitch. Jumping and pulling at the stud she will break the tie and could easily rupture him. Brace a tiny stud against your leg and put your other hand under his rump to support him. When tied to a bitch, some tiny studs never do turn back to back as larger studs will do. This is correct and is a good mating, and if he prefers to keep this stance with his front feet on the bitch's back facing in the same direction that she is, let him. But if he struggles and tries to turn around away from her, carefully take the hind leg in the direction that he is turning and lift it over her back to complete his turn. Prop rugs or towels under him to give him a firm footing; also, be sure that there is no strain or pull on his genitals.

The tie lasts from a few seconds to thirty-five or forty minutes, so this is another reason for you to sit on the floor. When the tie breaks, the stud will pull away from the bitch, showing you that the mating is completed. Hold the bitch upside down in your arms for several minutes to prevent her from urinating. Check the stud carefully to be certain hairs are away and penis is properly sheathed. Put the dogs in separate cages with fresh water to rest.

The usual procedure in mating Yorkies is to breed one day, rest the stud the next day and breed again the following day. This is done because you may have picked the wrong day for mating and it gives you a second chance for puppies. One completed mating is actually all that is necessary for a bitch to conceive.

Keep the bitch separated from any males after she is bred, until you can be sure her season is over. She could be mated again five or six days later and conceive puppies from both matings. If puppies were conceived and whelped from matings this close together, the ones from the second mating could be malformed or weak and not survive. Any animal who delivers multiple whelps can be mated by two or more studs at different times during one season unless care is taken to protect them.

CHAPTER 8

Prenatal, Whelping and Postnatal Care

You must take special care of your bitch during her pregnancy. Veterinarians say that the fetus of the puppy is completely formed during the first six weeks of pregnancy. Immediately following mating a bitch's intake of vitamins, minerals, calcium and proteins must be increased and her intake of starch foods cut down. If she will not eat raw ground beef, sauté it lightly in butter, corn oil or olive oil. Cook small amounts at a time so it is fresh and appealing to her. Fish and liver can be prepared the same way.

Divide one large meal a day into two smaller meals: one in the morning and one in the evening. Many Yorkies will not drink milk after they are weaned. If she will drink it, let her have all that she wants. Since fresh milk may give her loose bowels, give her canned evaporated milk half mixed with water and add a small amount of honey or Karo syrup for a treat.

Cheap calcium passes directly through the dog's body without being assimilated or absorbed, so the bitch receives no value from it. Get the best calcium that you can buy for her. I recommend Calcium Three with Vitamin D, made by the Gerard Pellham Pharmacal Company. This is a soft tablet, easy to give and highly assimilable. It is a real problem to get Yorkies to take the proper amounts of vitamins and minerals. Most good products are in powdered form and made for larger breeds. If you mix the specified amount of this powder with a Yorkie's food he will not eat it. Read formulas carefully before you buy any vitamin product and you will see that the more expensive vitamins are highly concentrated and thus a better buy for your Yorkie. I use Akti-Tabs, a conditioner and vitamin also from Pellham's. They are soft tablets, and my Yorkies eat them as they would candy treats—and they don't interfere with the meat meal of the dog.

If you have a special powdered vitamin and calcium that you have trouble giving your bitch, mix the required amount of the powder for the day with a small amount of milk or water. Add just enough liquid to make a thick paste. Put the paste on your thumb and insert it against the roof of her mouth. Pull your thumb out by scraping it against the underside of her teeth. The paste sticks to her teeth and the roof of her mouth and by the time she works it loose she has eaten it. Give her half of the paste in the morning and half at night.

She should continue to have regular exercise, but watch her carefully during the last few weeks of pregnancy to prevent jumping. About two weeks from whelping time the bitch will slow down physically and sleep more often. If her litter is large and she is uncomfortable, add a two- or three-inch solid foam rubber cushion to her bed. This is firm enough to support the weight of the puppies, yet soft enough to let her rest comfortably. A feather or chopped foam rubber cushion is not enough support. Be sure to slipcover the cushion with a pillowcase or towel so she will not chew the rubber. You may need to safety pin or sew the slipcover.

Average whelping time is sixty to sixty-three days from the day of mating, but a bitch will often whelp normally on the fifty-sixth or fifty-seventh day. If she was mated twice, this timing can be from either the first or second mating. Everything depends on the mating from which she conceived and when nature tells her the puppies are fully developed and ready to be born. Regardless of the day you have marked on your calendar, be patient and watch her for two or three days before the expected time. A first litter often comes several days earlier or later than the so-called "average" time of sixty days.

When the time is getting near, collect these items:

At least five or six old bath towels that you have sterilized
A pile of clean newspapers
A roll of dental floss
Grain alcohol to sterilize hands and instruments
A pair of blunt-nosed scissors
Sterile cotton and one-inch sterile gauze bandage
A box of cleansing tissues
A box of powdered alum

You may never use some of these, but if you need them to save the life of a puppy, you won't have time to go looking for them.

The best whelping box is a large cardboard cartoon about 18 by 24 inches and 20 inches high. Your grocer will have one. It is practical, safe for the puppies and can be destroyed when they are weaned. The large size is important because you can put an electric heating pad across the back of the box for the puppies, and the front half can be cooler for the bitch to rest in when she desires. Remove the entire lid from the box for easy access to the bitch and the puppies. You can cover the back half of the top with a blanket or towel to keep draft from the puppies and leave the front half uncovered for more air for the bitch.

With a large knife, cut a door in the front wall of the box large enough for the bitch to go in and out comfortably. Leave a four-inch sill at the bottom of this doorway. The bitch will step over the sill and it will keep the puppies from falling out. Put several layers of newspaper in the bottom of the box and place the heating pad across the back wall. Cover the pad with several more layers of paper and put a towel over all. Always have the heating pad turned to lowest heat for the comfort of the puppies.

On the fifty-fifth day take the bitch's temperature. It should be normal on this day. The normal temperature of a dog is 101.6° but this varies with different dogs, just as it does with humans. Keep a written record of temperature readings and take them regularly from now to whelping time. If you take a reading at 8:00 A.M., take it again at 8:00 P.M. or at any regular twelve-hour intervals. When her temperature starts to drop, you know she will whelp sometime within the next twenty-four hours. It will probably drop down into the nineties.

The day before whelping, a bitch often refuses food and empties her bowels several times to have them empty when she whelps. She may seem nervous and excited for a few hours, but as her time draws near she will want to sleep and her eyes will become dull and listless. Put her into the whelping box if she doesn't go in by herself. Most bitches will start tearing paper and arranging a nest for whelping, but some do not. This prelabor period can last an entire day or only a few hours, so watch carefully for her first bearing-down pains of hard labor. Make a note of the time hard labor begins. Exact knowledge of times may help your veterinarian save the life of a puppy or even the bitch's life. When he has exact times of events he knows if a situation is crucial or not or how much time he has to wait before it becomes crucial. He may give her injections to bring on labor or even perform a Caesarian if too much time has lapsed since her first pains.

A small bitch should never labor more than an hour without delivering a puppy. If she does, she may have a puppy caught in the birth canal at an odd angle where she cannot deliver it. In this case the veterinarian will try to turn the puppy so it can be delivered, and if it cannot be turned a Caesarian will probably be necessary.

Once heavy labor has started it should not stop for a long period of time. A bitch will rest between the delivery of each puppy, but when the puppy is cleaned and dry she should start labor again. If she does not, consult the veterinarian. After several heavy bearing-down pains the bitch should turn toward her vulva and chew at herself. The large, black bubble-like sac that appears under her tail is either the water sac preceding the puppy or the puppy itself. If a puppy is half in and half out of her body and she is having trouble delivering it, wrap a piece of towel around the puppy and grasp it firmly to keep it from returning into her body. Be gentle; do not jerk or pull roughly at the puppy, since it is easy to injure either it or the bitch. Keep a firm grasp on the puppy and gently work it back and forth from side to side as the bitch bears down with her pains. This should free the puppy.

The first puppy in a litter is often a dry birth since the water sac may have broken several hours before the puppy was on its way. When this happens there is not enough lubrication and the bitch will need help to dislodge the puppy. Hold the puppy with one hand and with the other hand carefully stretch the edges of the bitch's vulva away from the puppy as you would pull a glove from your hand. One or two slight pulls on the vulva will free the puppy. You must always help quickly in these situations because when a puppy is almost free of the bitch's body, you can be certain that the afterbirth has pulled away from the bitch's uterus and she is no longer furnishing the puppy with oxygen. The time has come for the puppy to start using his lungs. Up to this time he has been suspended in a water-tight sac completely surrounded with fluids and has been receiving oxygen through his navel cord. The sac surrounding the puppy must be broken away from his face to allow him to breathe and to drain the fluids away or he will drown in them when he tries to pull in air. Tear the sac away from his face with your fingers. It tears easily when you grasp it with both hands and pull away from the puppy.

An animal with multiple whelps may deliver as many breech births as head-first births. The head and shoulders are the largest part, so when they are presented first the bitch is stretched properly and the rest of the puppy just slips out. Breech births are more difficult because the tiny hind feet and legs come first and there is very little to grasp to help pull the puppy out. Also, the sac is now being torn from labor and the head of the puppy is still inside of the bitch's body.

When this happens you must work quickly, pulling gently on the cord which is attached to the puppy's stomach. The other end is fastened to the afterbirth and is inside of the bitch's body. Gently pull the cord, from the bitch's end, away from the puppy. You must pull enough cord out to cut, leaving a two- to four-inch length on the puppy or it will be disemboweled. When the cord is not too tightly fastened inside of the bitch, it pulls out easily to the point where you can cut it with the blunt-nosed scissors. If you have forceps, use them on the end of the cord to stop the bleeding; if not, tie a piece of dental floss near the end of the cord and as far away from the puppy's body as you can. The bitch will lick the cord, and if it is too close to the stomach she may hurt the puppy. If the cord is torn or too short to tie, put a pinch of powdered alum on it, but don't rub or touch the wound. Wrap a length of sterile bandage several times around the puppy's body and tie it loosely. Keep this bandage in place until you are certain the bleeding has stopped. If there is still bleeding, put more alum on the cord and rebandage.

When a cord is torn or cut, the afterbirth returns inside the bitch's body and her next labor pain should bring it out. Keep accurate count of the afterbirths as all must be delivered. If one is retained after whelping is finished it will cause a serious infection.

Most veterinarians tell you to take afterbirths away from the bitch. Wild animals used to eat them for the minerals and vitamins they provided that kept the bitch from having immediately to forage for food and leave her whelps. Your Yorkie does not need these, and even one afterbirth will upset her stomach and give her loose bowels for days. Wrap each one in tissue and flush it down the toilet. Each one is about half the size of a puppy and looks like a piece of dark liver. The medical term for it is the *placenta*.

Breech births, dry births and too short or torn cords cause the most problems. If you know about them they will be no problem for you.

When all goes well and the bitch does not want help, let her have her own way; but encourage her and watch carefully for any sign of trouble. Most Yorkies welcome help and learn to rely on you. If the bitch permits you to help, take the puppy and dry it carefully in a rough towel. Rub the excess moisture from it and at the same time massage its rib cage if the breathing is not strong. When the puppy is limp and grey and breathing is shallow, blow your breath gently into its mouth and nostrils to get more air into its lungs. This also helps to remove mucus from the nostrils. A strong, healthy puppy arrives crying lustily and sucking air into its lungs. The noiser they are for the first few minutes, the better.

Sometimes a bitch is tired and does not chew the cord to separate the afterbirth. When this happens, cut it carefully and leave the three or four inches hanging on the puppy with the dental floss on the end of it. Tie it tightly. The bitch licks the cord and it gradually dries up and drops off. Never pull it off.

When you are certain that all puppies are delivered and after-births accounted for, remove the wet towels and papers and replace them with dry ones. Under running warm water wash the excess dirt and blood from the bitch's hindquarters and nipples. Get her completely dry with towels and a hair dryer. Check the underside of her coat for hair mats. Comb them out and keep the long hair free and loose. If coat is exceptionally long and thick, wrap the hair in small bundles close to her body so there is no chance of a puppy hanging itself in a noose of hair made by a mat. Check for these mats every day.

Return her to the warm, dry whelping box with her puppies. Offer her water, milk and a small amount of food. She probably will not eat solid food but she should accept fluids, since her body is depleted from whelping.

Make certain that all puppies are nursing. If one is not, hold it up to a nipple and squeeze a few drops of milk onto its lips. This should start it nursing. Many puppies instinctively hunt for a nipple when they are barely outside the dam's body, while others do not start to nurse for an hour or more. If the puppy is active and not fretting, don't worry about it. If it is weak and limp, give it Esbilac mixed with water according to the instructions on the can. Give the puppy a few drops at a time until it is strong enough to nurse. The most important thing for the first few days is to see that the puppies are nursing. Also, keep them warm and out of **drafts.**

CHAPTER 9

Care of the Nursing Bitch—
Care and Development of Puppies

Newborn puppies nurse day and night the first few days of life and can double in size during this time. For this reason the bitch must have additional vitamins, calcium and good food to feed them properly. Feed her three or four times a day. She needs good protein such as beef, lightly cooked fish, liver, kidney and heart, and all the milk she will drink. A bitch with a fussy appetite who won't eat at this time is the one most likely to develop eclampsia, since there is too much of a calcium depletion by the puppies' nursing and not enough calcium intake.

Eclampsia, or milk-fever, as it is often called, is caused by lack of calcium or lack of calcium assimilation. The proper name for the condition is *puerperal tetany*, since it occurs during puerperium and is manifested by symptoms of tetany. I give the medical definition since it simplifies the description of what happens to the bitch. A novice might think that the bitch had been poisoned or had tetanus when they saw her in convulsions.

Watch for danger signs, as they appear in a matter of minutes. The bitch seems restless, pants and drinks excessive amounts of water. Her breasts and body become hot to the touch and her pulse races as her temperature rises. Slight muscular contractions start in her scalp and legs. As eclampsia advances, muscular contractions become violent and the bitch can no longer stand on her feet. When this happens at night and you do not hear her thrashing around, she may be unconscious and in delerium when you find her. Even if she is conscious, her eyes will be unfocused and she will be disoriented. The bitch must have immediate medical attention. The veterinarian will give her an intravenous injection of calcium and glucose to save her life. When the attack is violent or prolonged it may be hours before the convulsions stop and she returns to normal behavior.

When you bring her home she must rest and be kept quiet

The author's Dolly and Mitzi (with friend).

and away from her puppies, since she has been in extreme shock. Put her in another room where she will neither hear nor see the puppies, since her normal instinct is to go to them and nurse them, which would only bring on another, more severe attack of eclampsia. Start rubbing her breasts with cotton soaked in camphorated oil and continue doing so morning and night until the milk is dried up. If milk supply is excessive, you must apply hot packs to keep the breasts from swelling and bursting. Use a small, rough towel soaked in water as hot as she can comfortably stand. Apply these hot packs several times a day until the inflammation and swelling are gone.

Eclampsia occurs, as a rule, any time after the bitch starts to nurse the puppies. Usually it happens when the puppies are from ten days to two weeks old. Bitches with the larger milk supplies are more prone to eclampsia than bitches with a normal supply.

With a first litter the bitch's nipples are often tiny and inverted. Massage them with a small amount of vaseline and wipe off any excess. It may be necessary to do this several times before the nipples are out far enough for the puppies to nurse. If her milk supply is slow to come in and sparse at first, you may have to feed the puppies a few drops of Esbilac to strengthen them and keep them alive.

You should suspect they are not getting enough milk if they are fretful and cry often and their stomachs are bloated and rumbling. These noisy stomachs are due to either gas, diarrhea or a lack of food. Figure out which of these situations you have, because the problem could be that the bitch's milk is toxic to the puppies. When you suspect this, check immediately with your veterinarian. He will take the puppies away from the bitch and you will have to hand-feed them. These situations must be watched for since lack of food or diarrhea can dehydrate a puppy in a matter of hours and there is no way to save him when this happens.

With fretful puppies, try supplementing their food with an eyedropper and Esbilac during the day and see if the bitch can care for them at night. Often it is several days before she gets an adequate milk supply, so this method is best. Hand-feeding is dangerous and time-consuming, and they are still getting some of the bitch's milk.

When you hand-feed a litter, put a small mark on each puppy with nail polish. Mark each one in a different spot on its head or feet. This prevents you from missing one puppy at mealtime and feeding another twice, for they all look alike at night. Puppies must be fed every three hours around the clock during their first two weeks; after that every four hours is sufficient. Your only gauge of proper feeding is their general appearance and their bowel movements. When bowel movements are firm and regular and puppies are active, eating well and not fretting, you know that your feeding formula and timing is correct. Puppies sleep except when they are hungry, eating or need to have their body functions relieved. Watch them closely because a too quiet, limp puppy is more likely to be sick than one who cries and fusses. The limp one is too weak to cry and needs special care and extra feeding.

When bowels are loose, immediately change your feeding formula. Always try Esbilac first since most pet shops handle it and its formula is the closest one to bitch's milk. When Esbilac is not available or does not agree with a puppy, mix 1 large can of evaporated milk with 1 can of warm water, add the yolk only of 1 egg, 1 tablespoon of Karo syrup or honey and 1 tablespoon of lime water. Buy lime water at the drug store; you don't want lime juice. Mix all ingredients together and store in the refrigerator in a closed jar. When feeding puppies, remove only the amount

Wee Blue Mouse on and next to a slice of bread. Another Martello 1½ pounder.

of formula you need for one meal. Put it in a small bottle and heat this bottle in hot water just to body temperature. Do not let it boil or get too hot for the puppy to drink.

Wrap the puppy in a towel to get a firm grip and hold it erect when feeding. Until puppies are weaned their only method of eating is to suck strongly, so a puppy must be held erect to prevent it from sucking the formula into its lungs. From the dropper, carefully squeeze a few drops onto the end of the tongue. The puppy will cup its tongue and suck the formula down the throat. Don't let it grab the dropper or it will choke on an excess of liquid. If this accidentally happens, turn the puppy upside down (head down) and pat its shoulders to get liquid out and air in. You soon develop a sense of rhythm in feeding. By putting one drop on the tongue as the puppy swallows one drop, he will push against your hand with his paw just as though he were nursing on his dam.

Puppies cannot urinate without your help for the first few weeks, and they will die if they are not helped. When the dam is caring for them there is no problem, as she cleans them with her tongue, but when you are feeding them clean them after each feeding. Dampen a piece of cotton with warm water and rub it gently over the puppy's privates. One drop of urine at a time will well up on the puppy and you wipe the urine away with the damp cotton. You must do this until the puppy is on its feet and you see that it can urinate without help.

Bowels usually move without help but here too you can help with damp cotton if the puppy is straining and producing poor results. When bowel movement is jammed against the rectum you must help remove it. If the puppy strains and has had no movement for over a day, take another eyedropper and put 6 or 8 drops of glycerin in the tube and gently squeeze this into the puppy's rectum. Do *not* insert the dropper deeply, but just inside of the rectum. The puppy should have a bowel movement within a minute since the glycerin creates a drawing action as well as lubrication. This method for helping constipation is for the lower bowels only, that is, if you see a movement just inside of the puppy which is pressing to get out but won't come. If you are not familiar with this method you should ask your veterinarian if you may use it. Never give a nursing puppy a laxative of any form or any medication that your veterinarian does not give you.

During hand-feeding you should keep a written record on each puppy. This is a simple thing since you have marked the puppies. Record each feeding time, bowel movement, etc., so you know exactly how each puppy has been cared for and how it is progressing. This helps your veterinarian if one puppy gets sick.

Yorkies are born with long, tapering tails, black on the top side with a V-shaped tan marking on the underside. Tails should be docked and dewclaws removed at four to six days of age. If puppies are weak or ill your veterinarian will want to postpone this. If he is not familiar with the breed, have him dock the tail at the end of the tan V on the underside just inside the black hairs. This V is wide at the rectum and tapers to a point about one third the length of the tail. This way he leaves all of the tan hairs and a few black ones on the remaining tail stub. It is better to dock a tail too long than to ruin a dog by docking it too short. The longer tail can be corrected when the dog is older.

The puppies' eyes open from nine to fourteen days after birth. When you are caring for them, keep the corners of the eyes and the edges of the eyelids clean with cotton soaked in a solution of warm water and weak boric acid. Eyelids are sticky when eyes are opening and you must keep them clean if the dam is not caring for them.

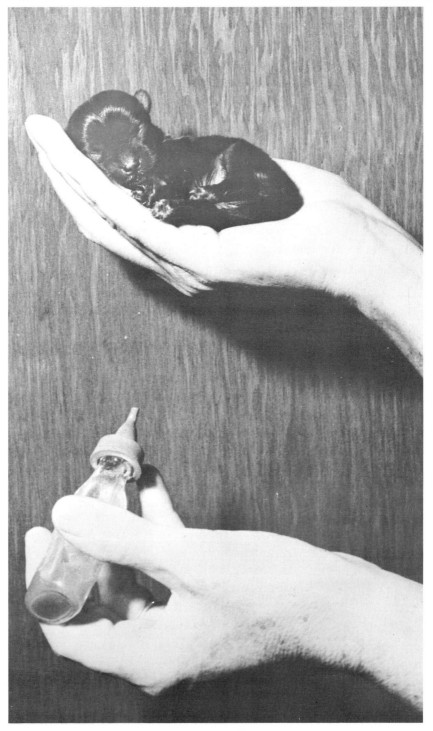

The author's Tiny Tim at 5 days. He weighed 1½ lbs. full grown.

Puppies usually walk by two to three weeks of age and by four weeks they are stronger on their feet and need more room for exercise. Take them from the brood box and put them in a confined area, which you can make with a circle of fence wire cut to the height that you want. In one corner put a small stool for the bitch to use in jumping in and out of the pen. Be sure the puppies are out of danger and drafts; in winter put a small cardboard box on its side for a shelter. Put a heating pad inside and cover it with bedding. Puppies soon learn to crawl to this warm bed to sleep.

Start to wean them by pouring a small amount of Esbilac or milk formula in a flat saucer and mix Pablum with it to make a thick paste. Puppies wade in it, fall in it and generally mess themselves up, but they manage to eat more of it if it is thick when they are learning to lap food. As they grow, make the mixture thinner with more liquid and less cereal. Remove the dish after each feeding and sponge the puppies off with a damp washcloth before you return them to the pen. Brush the coat to be certain it is dry. This is also the time to bathe their privates and check for bowel movements which can be stuck under their tails. Vaseline will heal any urine burns on their stomachs.

Trim excess hair from the edges and inside and outside of the ears just as soon as it starts to grow. With a thick coat, this trimming should start when they are a few days old. An excess of hair on the ears will keep them from lifting properly. At the same time keep the tiny needle-like toenails clipped. Puppies play roughly and can easily injure each other with these nails. If you start clipping nails and trimming ear hair even before their eyes are open, they never fear this grooming as they get older. Get them used to lying on their backs to be brushed even before they have hair and they will love it.

Feed puppies four to six weeks old every four hours; six weeks to four months, four times a day; four months to a year, three times a day; then feed as grown dogs.

Feed weaned puppies small amounts of good raw or cooked ground beef, Gerber's baby meats, milk and Pablum. All solid food should be fed in small amounts, in tiny pieces and in small dishes to keep it fresh and clean. Yorkie puppies eat often but they eat such small amounts that you must adjust to what they eat and need. Place the soft Gerber's meat in small gobs around the edge of a flat saucer so puppies can reach it easily without wading in it. When they are steadier on their feet, leave the dish of milk and Pablum and a dish of water in their pen at all times.

Never fail to get their immunization injections at the proper time to protect them from distemper, hepatitis and leptospirosis. As soon as the puppies are weaned, check with your veterinarian as to the proper time. These injections are the only life insurance your puppies have, so never let them grow or leave your home without this protection. Also, give a record of these immunizations to the new owner when you sell them.

Socialization of puppies is extremely important to their characters and personalities. As soon as they open their eyes, talk to them and love them each time you handle them, and soon they will respond and look for you. As they grow older, get them used to people and normal noises so they will take these for granted when they are mature. Puppies who have love and affection at an early age never fear people, nor are they puppies who run and hide and wet when they hear noises or a stranger approaches. Puppies without love are those that develop into the snarling ones with snapping dispositions, not because they are mean, but simply because they are afraid.

If a puppy is well and strong and going to be a pet in a home, it can leave you at three months, but if it is sold as show quality or breeding stock you should keep it longer so you know that it will fill these requirements.

Many changes take place in a Yorkie from four to seven months of age. His permanent teeth come in and the shape of his mouth often changes. Most puppies drop coats and start their new coats during this period. Ears are up and down as they cut teeth. The body and legs take on their permanent shapes. After seven months there is little change in a Yorkie other than an increase in size and weight and growth of coat. During his period of transition from puppy to dog, you discover that a puppy with short legs and a heavy body is more likely to have weak leg tendons than a cobby-bodied puppy with a bit more length of leg. The puppy's legs must be protected since these tendons are tiny, some not much thicker than a thread. Even puppies born with strong legs can have the tendons harmed if they are dropped, if the puppy jumps too much at an early age or if he slips on slippery floors when he is learning to walk. Try to protect him from such problems.

The puppy's mature body should be as nearly square as possible, with body sound and solid and as long as the dog is tall.

Milk teeth, or baby teeth, often fail to loosen and drop out as they should and a puppy will have a double set of teeth. These doubles usually occur in the area of the four fang teeth and the tiny upper and lower teeth across the front of the mouth. By six months these double teeth should be gone. When they stay in longer they start to grow roots which weaken the permanent teeth and often ruin the shape of the dog's mouth. Try to loosen the baby teeth by moving them back and forth with your fingers. The baby fangs are small and have a hook on the end, and the permanent teeth coming in are wide and straight. If the baby teeth are firm and deep-set, your veterinarian will have to remove them. When they are extremely long-rooted and difficult to pull, he may have to make a small slit in the puppy's gum to loosen the tooth, let the puppy rest a week and then pull the tooth.

A general anesthetic should never be given to pull these baby teeth, nor later on to have teeth cleaned. Yorkies as a breed are extremely sensitive to any general anesthetic, especially to any of the barbiturates, such as pentathol. Many Yorkies die every year from anesthetics given for pulling teeth and cleaning teeth.

If it seems cruel to you to have baby teeth pulled without an anesthetic, remember what my veterinarian told me. He said that it does hurt the puppy for a few minutes, but it is better to give the puppy this short term of pain than to walk out with a dead puppy in your arms. Strangely enough, much of the trouble is due to fright rather than pain, because you can hand a puppy a bone minutes after teeth have been pulled and he will grab it and start chewing, all thought of pain and discomfort gone.

CHAPTER 10

Coat Colors and Textures

Since Yorkies are noted for their beautifully colored, luxurious coats, color and texture of hair are two of the most important things for you to know about.

The texture of their hair is said to be the nearest thing to human hair found on any dog. This is true in many ways: the Yorkie's hair grows long and silky, it does not shed continuously as it does on many short-haired dogs, some hair is baby-fine and thin and other hair is thicker with more body. Just as with human hair, the thicker, stronger hair is more easily managed.

The reason for the difference in texture and color in Yorkie coats is quite logical. The breed was planned and "made" by breeding long-haired, soft-coated dogs with short-haired, coarse-coated dogs. Some were black, some white or light tan, and others were blue. From these combinations of coats and colors came our present-day Yorkie, so it is reasonable that certain strains or blood-lines carry one kind of coat while other strains have a different kind of coat. Colors vary accordingly.

All Yorkie puppies are born black and tan and short-haired and look more like Manchester Terriers or Doberman Pinschers than the glamorous, long-haired dogs they will be at maturity. Often this is a shock to the owner of a first litter. Yorkie hair starts to grow at two or three days of age. If you watch a litter closely, coat changes are visible from week to week. It is impossible to evaluate a litter properly at an early age. Often the beautiful puppy at five to six weeks of age will be the poorest puppy at nine to ten months. This is the reason that breeders who show their Yorkies do not sell them until they are from twelve to eighteen months old. Always remember that there are exception to all rules concerning any livestock, but here are a few guidelines to help you roughly evaluate your puppies for color when they are three to four months old.

When the tan has been bright and profuse on the head, chest and legs since birth, you may expect the puppies to have a clear golden tan at maturity. Little change takes place in this shade of tan; it keeps increasing in length and improving in color. If heads at this age are still black with little tan showing on head, chest or legs, they may never break to a proper tan but always have a dark, sooty tan streaked with black. Also, if the black head does break to the usual tan, it will go through a period of being a very pale tan which is almost white or grey. With this kind of tan break you will first notice the golden tan coming in at the base of the ears and around the muzzle at the roots of the grey hair. This shade of tan break happens often and usually clears to the desired lovely shaded golden tan at maturity.

Color break on the body from black to deep steel-blue takes place from three months on. It should not start to break this early though; when it does, you usually have a light silver-blue coat at maturity. A proper body color break should start from eight to ten months, underneath the coat and close to the body on the legs. Next it shows clearly in the center part on the spine. The color change is so gradual that often you do not notice it until you bathe the dog. A dark steel-blue coat rarely changes color completely until the dog is from two to three years old, but there is evidence of the coming change in color at the roots of the hair from ten months on.

When a puppy is three or four months old, you can also determine approximately what type and texture of coat it will have at maturity. If the hair is thick, black and silky but very fine and exceptionally long for his age, you have a producer of luxurious coats. The two disadvantages that often come with this kind of coat are that the body coat may remain coal-black and never break to deep steel-blue, or it may develop a wave or kink that cannot be brushed out. The kinky hair usually occurs on the hindquarters. With this coat the dog has a very black head with little tan showing from the time he is born.

Another kind of coat is composed of thin, sparse hair. It tangles and breaks easily. This coat is shed as a puppy coat from four to six months and the color break comes as the new coat comes in. It seldom grows to the correct length and density, but if it is the exception and does develop into a thick coat, it is usually light blue and tan.

Still another kind is wiry and coarse, especially the black hair. This hair remains coarse, breaks easily and never grows to any length.

The preferred coat is thick, silky, glossy and still black at four to six months. There is more body and density to the hair than in the soft, too-fine, black silky coat, but it is not coarse. This coat is often shed as a puppy coat but usually it just keeps growing. With grooming it grows longer and thicker as the dog matures. Color changes in this type take place from ten months to as long as two years, but once the deep steel-blue comes in it stays for many years without fading like the lighter blue coats.

If this breed is new to you or if you know nothing about the ancestors of one or both dogs who produced the litter, you can see why it is to your advantage to keep the puppies until you can properly evaluate them. Many changes in color and coat take place during the first year of a Yorkie's life.

CHAPTER 11

Bathing, Grooming and Wrapping Coats

If your Yorkie is just a pet and friend and you do not care about length of coat, he is no more difficult to bathe and care for than any other dog. But if you want to have a lovely, long coat, either for show or for your personal satisfaction, there are many things you will need to know. Here is a basic list of things to get together before you start the bath:

A soft, short-toothed nylon comb for dealing with most tangles.

A long-toothed steel comb for making the center back part and unraveling the more serious tangles.

A soft, natural bristle brush with the longest bristles you can find. This is for grooming; it polishes and shines the coat.

A small, rat-tailed natural bristle brush with short bristles for grooming whiskers and feet

A good shampoo that does not have a detergent base. I recommend Gerard Pellham Pharmacal's shampoo and rinses or Breck's shampoo for dry hair.

A creme rinse, either from Pellham or Breck, diluted per instructions.

If possible, bathe your Yorkie in a deep laundry tray so that he is safe from slipping. Place a piece of old terry cloth towel or washcloth on the bottom of the tray for him to stand on. He will not be afraid if he has a firm footing.

Bathe his ears inside and out with a washcloth, shampooing and carefully rinsing so as to keep excess water from his ears. Dry partially and put small wads of cotton in his ears before wetting his entire head. Wash his head, keeping soap out of his eyes but being sure to soak the corners of his eyes where there may be a discharge. Rinse his head carefully and towel-dry away excess water. Then wet his entire body, being careful to keep the back center part in place. Rub shampoo gently onto the body, legs and underside, always working away from the center part on his back. By doing this you keep the hair so trained to the part that it will be almost impossible to part the hair off center.

Rinse all suds from the body with a spray of warm water. If you do not have a spray, make certain that all suds are out of the coat by pouring cups of warm water over the dog. Pour the diluted creme rinse on his body, gently working it through his coat. Rinse this out with warm water. Carefully towel-dry the excess water from him, putting him on a table where you can sit beside him and work with the coat as you dry it. A small portable electric hair dryer with heat and blower action is ideal. I recommend the Oster Airjet Model 202, since it is lightweight and sits on a stand, thus leaving both hands free to work with the coat. Be careful that the heat is not too near the coat, as the flying hair can easily be burned. A small electric heater can also be used but is more dangerous.

Brush the hair up, away from the body, so that the heat will reach the coat close to the body. Keep turning and brushing him as you dry him all over. At the same time loosen any tangles with your fingers and brush them out. A tangle usually loosens with brushing after you have separated the main tangle with your fingers. However, if one is stubborn you will have to get it out with a comb. Always use the short-toothed soft comb first, and then, as a last resort, the long-toothed steel one.

When the dog is dry and free of tangles, cut his toenails and remove excess hair from between the pads of his feet. Food and sticky things collect there, and if they catch in the hair they cause a painful lump. Also, cut long hair from the top and around the edges of the foot to make it appear neat and round. Don't chop the hair off; cut a small amount at a time and try to layer it for a smooth look. Trim hair from edges and the inside and outside of the ears about halfway down the ear.

Good coat conditioners are a must for grooming and coat growing. I recommend Pellham's Whisper Spray for everyday use and finishing touches and St. Aubrey's Royal Coatalin for heavy duty hair care. Whisper is a light, penetrating oil that nourishes the hair and leaves it with a sheen but no greasy deposit. Heavy oil preparations actually harm a Yorkie's coat since they mat hair. Also, they cause him discomfort and are cold on his body in the winter.

Use the heavy conditioner sparingly. Start by putting a small amount on the fingers and palm of one hand. Rub your hands together to spread into a thin film and gently work this into the hair. Brush, add more conditioner and brush again. If the hair still seems dry, repeat the full procedure. When a thin spray oil is used it can be sprayed directly on the coat and brushed in.

As soon as a puppy has enough hair on his head to make a small topknot, start putting it up. Early wrapping of the hair protects it and encourages its growth. The whiskers will be next to wrap. If they are not protected they drag through the food, milk and water, and either your dog himself or another puppy will chew them off as they play. Watch him when you start wrapping whiskers, as he may try to chew the wrappers off. To discourage this practice, moisten a small amount of cayenne pepper, or use a drop of hot sauce, and put it on the wrappers. Use this similarly on wrappers that he tries to chew on any part of his body. The younger the dog is when the first wrappers are put on him, the less trouble you will have as you add more to wrap a full coat.

If you are planning to show your Yorkie, you will have to separate him from other puppies. Nothing will destroy a coat faster than two puppies romping and playing together and chewing at each other. Many people cage a Yorkie when they plan to show him simply to protect the coat. This is a cruel thing to do to such an energetic little dog who is full of love and life, and with ordinary precautions it is not necessary. When you have other Yorkies in your home, it is always wise to separate the wrapped dogs before you leave the house. Left alone, they play roughly.

You must check the corners of his eyes and mouth every morning and wash away any discharge from the eyes or any food from the whiskers and mouth. Carefully soak the matter loose with a washcloth or cotton and warm water. Brush it out with the small bristle brush, or if necessary, use the fine-toothed end of the soft nylon comb. Eye corners and mouth corners are the points where hair loss is the greatest, but they are the starting places for the beautiful long golden-tan moustache and head-fall which add so much to the Yorkshire Terrier's appearance.

Coat wrapping was done in the past with soft strips of old silk or linen cloth. If you have any, try them. Most breeders today use strips of heavy waxed paper of the type used by florists. The wrappers used for a full coat usually include one for the topknot, one on each side of the mouth for whiskers, four on each side of the body, one on each hind leg and one on the tail. As the coat grows in length and thickness, add wrappers on front legs, chest, and underside. With a puppy, use only one wrapper, that on the topknot.

Before you start wrapping, cut wrappers into strips two inches wide and of varying lengths, from four inches for the short coat to longer strips as required for the side coat. All wrappers must cover the hair to be wrapped and extend in length past the ends of the hair. This protects the hair and keeps it from matting and breaking. When you wrap a coat a few times, you will know exactly what size wrappers offer the best coat protection for your dog. Some will need to be wider and longer and some can be shorter. There is no fixed figure on how many wrappers you will need or what length they should be. You discover the answer to this with practice, for no two Yorkies have exactly the same amount of coat.

Carefully part the hair to be wrapped with a comb, work a small amount of coat conditioner into the hair and brush it well. Be careful that strands from one wrapping do not pull against the

Two views showing area on ears where hair should be trimmed, and how to part hair on head.

one next to it, and do not wrap too close to the body. (Drawing shows you that the wrappings hang loosely from the body.) Fold the wrapper lengthwise and crease it with your fingers. Then, holding the wrapper in one hand, place the hair length inside against the center crease, making sure that the wrapper extends past the ends of the hair. Fold the wrapper and hair lengthwise once again. This lengthwise double fold keeps the hair straight and keeps it from tangling. Starting at the hair and wrapper ends, fold up toward the body in folds of one or two inches until it is in a neat bundle and swinging loosely, as illustrated. Wrap a small rubber band around the center of the bundle several times to secure it.

A wrapped coat.

When wrapping hair on the back legs, be sure that the hair is not pulled so tight that the dog cannot walk or sit down easily. Also, the wrapper on the tail must have the rubber band around the hair and bundle only, and not up on the tail itself. The rubber band can stop circulation in the tail, causing it to die and drop off.

Wrappers sometimes split, and the hair gets soiled or matted, so you must take all wrappers down every two or three days and brush the hair free of dirt and tangles. Then apply a small amount of coat conditioner, brush well and rewrap. The more you brush, the more the coat grows, so do not neglect this part of grooming.

Some Yorkies are confirmed scratchers for no reason at all. They will sit and scratch at the hair and wrappers. This must be stopped at once or the dog will cause more damage by matting and tearing the hair than if the coat had not been wrapped at all. For this problem, try putting boots on his hind feet. This may cure him of the scratching habit. If it does not, you will have to put boots on him every time he is wrapped.

To make boots, buy seamless tubular surgical gauze from a surgical supply house. This is a tubular bandage made for bandaging fingers and toes and comes in a roll. Size #2 is best for most Yorkies, but if your dog is large, ask for a larger size.

For your first boot, cut a piece of gauze about six inches long from the roll. Stretch it over two fingers on one hand, putting your fingers about halfway down the length of the gauze. Twist the remaining gauze in a complete turn at the end of your fingers to close the opening. Pull this remaining gauze inside out and up over the fingers to the starting point, making a little boot. It takes a few tries to make you an expert at this operation! You may have to cut a longer length if you need a longer boot to fit your Yorkie's foot, but this six-inch length is a good size to try for the first time. Put the boot on his hind foot and tie it in place with a soft tape or piece of cloth, just above the joint of his foot. Don't let the boot be so short that it pulls, and don't tie it too tight—just tight enough to keep it in place without dropping off. If he is always in the house, a pair of boots will last him a week or more.

If you brush and groom attentively, it is not necessary to bathe your Yorkie so often. A good rule is to bathe only when the dog needs it because he is messy or dirty, or because you are taking him to a show. The Yorkie does not have a body odor as some breeds do, so the brushing and grooming keeps him clean as you are growing coat and keeps his skin pliable.

A male dog must have the urine carefully washed from his side coat before it is wrapped. Wash him with a washcloth and warm water and rinse the urine-soaked hair until it is free of any stickiness and odor. By keeping this side coat wrapped, you prevent urine breakage of the hair and keep a cleaner little dog. If he does get urine on the wrapper, change it at once, before it soaks to the hair, and reposition it where it will keep dry.

If you do not wrap your Yorkie it is still important to brush him and free his hair from tangles every few days. This takes only a few minutes. When you permit tangles to stay in the coat, they go deeper and deeper into the coat until they form a mat against the body that is impossible to comb out without cutting off the entire coat. It is like a tight suit of armor against his body.

In summer, dry and groom his coat outdoors in the sun. It is done in half the time, especially if there is a light breeze. In cold weather, pick a nice warm spot in the house where the sun shines through the window. He will love the sunshine, and it always seems to add luster and color to his coat.

Once the grooming and wrapping becomes a routine it takes only a few minutes, so don't be discouraged if it takes a long time at the start. It is well worth the trouble when you see the progress that you make in growing coat.

The English used to say that it was brushing and elbow grease that made lovely Yorkie coats rather than any preparation of grease that you used.

CHAPTER 12

Feeding Your Yorkshire Terrier

A balanced diet of good food is essential to the health of any living creature. It is easier to feed properly several Yorkies than it is to feed one small, spoiled Yorkie. With only one, he is more likely to get what he wants by turning up his nose at the proper food. If this happens he will be a picky eater who is not properly nourished.

Naturally your puppy wants to eat exactly what you do, and he will often beg for the things that are not good for him. If you are wise you will start him on good eating habits early and keep him on a routine feeding plan. You will have a healthier, happier dog with strong bones and good teeth.

Lean ground beef is a good basic diet. Often he will eat a few bites of it raw for his morning snack. For basic meals, sear a small amount of beef very lightly in a skillet with a small amount of olive oil, corn oil or low-fat cooking oil. Add one part of cooked rice or a fine-kibbled puppy meal to two parts of beef and a small amount of powdered skim milk. If you feed a powdered or granular vitamin, such as Aktigen, add the proper amount at the last minute, remove from the fire and cover with a lid. Let it stand at least ten minutes to blend and to soften the meal. The percentage of powdered skim milk is one-half cup to one pound of meat.

There are now many nutritional kibbles and puppy meals on the market. These are formulated by animal nutritionists and contain a good balance of vitamins and minerals essential to your dog's health. They should be fed in small amounts along with good meat but not alone with water, as many manufacturers recommend. A Yorkie is small; he does not eat much, since he doesn't have much room, and he does require meat. With meat alone, however, you have problems with bones and early loss of teeth, so you can see that meat, kibble or cereal and vitamins are all necessary and should be fed together. Once your Yorkie is used to either the rice or small kibble, you can change his menu by using lamb, boneless fish, canned tuna fish or chicken in place of the beef in his main meal. Just before you serve it spread vitamin and coat oil such as Aktoleum, in the required amount, over his meal.

Other foods to feed him are cottage cheese, small amounts of crisp bacon, kidney, liver and brains. Too much liver will give him loose bowels. When a dog has been ill and is recovering he will often eat these organ meats raw, in small amounts. They digest more easily than when they are cooked.

It is always good to keep on hand a few cans of good dog food, such as Alpo, Purina or Gaines. These come in a variety of good solid meats and are not just "fillers," as so many cheap canned foods are. Gainsburgers or Gaines' Variety Pack of Prime and small jars of Gerber's baby meats are also a healthy standby. If you don't have time to cook or are traveling with your dog, all of these products are ready to use and convenient to carry with you. It is wise to get him used to these different foods at an early age.

Don't feed him sausage, pork, spiced luncheon meat, weiners, corned beef or highly seasoned foods. Never let him have turkey bones, chicken bones or any type of fowl bones. These bones splinter, and slivers from them can catch in his throat or intestines and kill him. Be certain that any bone you give him is too large to allow him to get the entire thing in his mouth. He loves to drag large bones around and chew on them. For a special treat have a shinbone with marrow sawed into circles about an inch thick. He will eat the marrow and play with the bone ring for days.

Few Yorkies drink milk after they are weaned, but if your Yorkie does, let him have a small dish every day. He will be more likely to drink canned milk half mixed with water than whole milk. Also, whole milk will often give him diarrhea. A puppy must have additional calcium while he is growing. It is essential to his general health, bones and teeth. I give and recommend Calcium Three With D from Gerard Pellham Pharmacal Company. This company makes all of the body-conditioning vitamins and coat oils that I feed my Yorkies.

The calcium is in a soft tablet that is easily broken and contains highly assimilable calcium. If you have a problem giving him his calcium, or any pill, you can always wrap a small amount of Underwood's canned liver sausage spread around the pill and he gobbles up the "treat" without knowing the pill was there.

Another problem you may find with a Yorkie is that he will refuse to eat food which has vitamins mixed in with it. Since the amount of food consumed is so small, don't try to force something on him that he won't eat. In this case you can give him his vitamin conditioner in the form of Akti-Tabs. These soft tablets are easily broken. Not only are they high in vitamin content, but the flavor appeals to all dogs. Tiny puppies who can barely walk and who have no teeth will eat small pieces of them.

For treats give him small milk-bone biscuits to chew on, marrowbones, or desiccated liver tablets that you can purchase from a health food store. Do not give him candy in any form. Some Yorkies will eat a small piece of apple, orange or pear and this will not hurt him.

A Yorkie of two pounds or less has a very small stomach, but he still has a lot of energy to be built up. It is wise, therefore, to feed him small amounts and at more frequent intervals than you would feed a larger Yorkie. I have found over the years that these tiny ones do want to eat more than twice a day, and they require it to keep up their health and energy.

I mention these different methods of feeding since this is a problem that you have to work out the first few weeks you have your puppy. The tiny ones are the ones that find it most difficult to adjust to a proper feeding program, so be sure that they have small amounts of food at frequent intervals so the food will be fresh.

The morning meal for any Yorkie can be a dish of milk, a milk-bone, a few bites of egg or bacon and his vitamin tablet. This will get his little motor started for the day.

Once you find a sensible feeding program and one that you know nourishes him you will have no problem. Most Yorkies are good eaters; the only people with a problem eater are the ones who let the puppy have his own way in the beginning.

CHAPTER 13

First Aid and Glossary

In an emergency you want immediate help. I have written this chapter in an informal manner to give you that help.

The glossary of terms will serve as a quick reference when the need arises. Many of the terms explained here will be found in illustrations throughout the book.

ANESTHETIC—Yorkies are extremely sensitive to any general or barbiturate-type anesthetic. Anesthesia should never be given by weight to a Yorkie but only by the "to effect method." This means start with small amount and give only what is absolutely needed to obtain the proper effect.

ANAL GLANDS—Empty these by holding raised tail in one hand and gently squeezing glands located on either side of rectum. They empty through the rectum. If abnormally painful and red or swollen, consult veterinarian.

APPLE HEAD—Round, high-domed head as in Toy Spaniels. Not desirable in Yorkies.

BARLEY WATER—This is strengthening and easy to digest when a puppy is weak, dehydrated and barely able to swallow. Simmer 2 oz. pearl barley in 1 qt. water for 2 hrs. Strain immediately to rid of lumps and hulls. One-quarter honey to three-quarter barley water may be supplemented and fed with dropper or spoon. Good after fever, sore throat or diarrhea. Keep refrigerated, as it spoils rapidly.

BAT EARS—Ears very round on top. Too large and widespread, although may be erect. Not desirable in Yorkies.

BEDDING—Soft wool and many modern fabrics, especially carpeting, break off coat. Use toweling or a soft cushion covered with fabric without a long nap.

BONE SWALLOWED—Reach finger in mouth and try to hook finger in back of bone to pull out. If bone is out of reach and you know it is small, give the dog balls of soft bread to ease the bone loose. He will either swallow or throw up the bone. If bone is a larger one, turn dog upside down and pat briskly on back to dislodge. If dog still gags, get vet.

BUTTERFLY NOSE—Mottled in color. Not entirely black as should be and usually shows brown or pink spots.

CAMELBACK—Convex back, roached and higher in the middle. Opposite of swayback.

CAT FOOT—Short, round and compact foot like a cat. Desirable in Yorkies.

COBBY—Short, compact body. Also called short-coupled or close-coupled. Desirable in Yorkies.

CONSTIPATION—Small piece of soap shaved to a point and inserted gently just inside rectum, or ½ eyedropper of pure glycerin will relieve tightly packed lower bowels. Also, a few drops of milk of magnesia given orally, in small amounts only.

CONVULSIONS—Put dog in small, warm box in quiet room. Try to find cause to explain to vet if they do not stop. When caused by overexcitement or extremely hot weather during teething time, it is over quickly. If vomiting occurs suspect poison and get vet.

COW-HOCKED—Hocks bent inward, throwing hind feet out incorrectly.

CRYPTORCHID—Usually a male with no testicles descended into the scrotum. Male not entire. A fault.

DEWCLAWS—Extra fifth toe or claw on puppy. Usually on front feet only but does occur on back feet. Have removed when tail is docked.

DIARRHEA—In tiny puppies must be stopped immediately as puppy will dehydrate if attack is violent. Often happens mildly in change of home, food and water. Small amounts of Parepectolin or Kaopectate from dropper should help after few doses every hour. If it does not stop or puppy is weak and limp, consult vet.

DUDLEY NOSE—Flesh-colored or yellowish-brown in spots. Usually comes with light eyes and eye rims. Not desirable in Yorkies.

ECLAMPSIA—See chapter 9.

ELBOW—Top joint of front leg where it joins the shoulder blade.

FEISTY—Aggressive temperament.

FIDDLE FRONT—Bandy-legged with legs bowed out at elbows. Usually denotes loose muscles in joints. Not desirable in Yorkies.

FLEAS—Use mild aerosol spray or mild medicated shampoo put out by Pellham Pharmacal. Does the job without destroying coat.

Avoid flea powder since most contain abrasives that cut coat.

FLOP EARS—Broad ears falling to the sides of the head and not erect.

GAS PAINS—Dog lies stretched out to full length trying to ease pains. Rumbling in intestines is audible. Give small amount of Parepectolin or Pepto-Bismol. Hold dog on your shoulder and gently rub stomach. If condition worsens or dog gets weak and limp, consult vet immediately since dog may have eaten something toxic. In tiny puppies this can cause shock since gas presses against heart.

GAY TAIL—Tail carried either too erect or tilted back toward the head. Not desirable in Yorkies.

HERNIA—Protrusion of the intestine through the abdominal cavity walls. At navel is called *umbilical hernia;* in groin, an *inguinal hernia.* Always consult vet as it can be extremely dangerous.

HEIGHT—Measure from level line over shoulders to ground.

HOCKS—Joints in hind legs between the pasterns and the stifles.

HYDROCEPHALUS—Called "water on the brain." Usually in very young, unweaned puppies but can show up later. Puppy staggers as if head too heavy to hold up. Head is heavy, overround on top and larger than normal in size; eyes protrude. Consult vet.

HYPOGLYCEMIA—Usually in small puppies but does occur in grown toy breeds. An acute low blood sugar condition caused by some form of stress. Often diagnosed as acute hepatitis or brain damage if vet does not have enough information about attack. Puppy is limp and semiconscious and mouth and gums are grey. Improper elimination, improper feeding, lack of food, overeating or too much handling and lack of rest often cause this in a healthy puppy. Consult vet immediately and give *Shock formula* (which see).

LEGGY—Legs too long and make dog appear to be out of proportion.

LENGTH OF DOG—Measured from shoulder at base of neck to base of tail. Yorkies should be square in body, approximately as high as they are long.

LOIN—Back part of body between last rib and hip joint.

MONORCHID—Usually a term used when male has only one testicle descended into scrotum. Dog not complete. Vets use the terms *monorchid* and *cryptorchid* when referring to one or both testicles not descended. A fault that occurs in many toy breeds. Can be hereditary but is not always.

MORBID APPETITE—All puppies chew on wood and hard objects when cutting teeth, but if they eat small stones and bits of wood when past teething stage suspect worms or extreme vitamin deficiency.

OVERSHOT MOUTH—Upper teeth protrude over front lower teeth. Usually caused by misshapen jaw. A fault to breed away from.

PASTERN—Lower part of leg, below the knee on foreleg or below the hock on hind leg.

PATELLA—Kneecap.

PRICK EARS—Ears tapering to a point and carried stiffly erect.

ROACHBACK—Convex curvature of the back. Also called camelback or humpback.

SECOND THIGH—Also called lower thigh; the hind leg between stifle joint and the hock.

SEDATIVES—Very dangerous to Yorkies. Should never be given without vet's authority and then in extremely small amounts.

SHOCK—If dog is dropped, hits head, is sick from heat or lack of air, it goes into shock. Dog is limp, semiconscious, eyes unfocused, gums and tongue are grey. Breathing is shallow and heartbeat is weak and uneven. Hold dog's head up so he will not choke and insert ½ eyedropper *Shock formula* (which see) inside cheek. Hold mouth shut and gently rub throat to make him swallow. Also massage rib cage while holding him on your shoulder to aid breathing. Wrap him in wool for warmth since body heat drops rapidly. Keep hands away from top of head as he may have a concussion from hitting his head. If cause was simple this will bring him around in about 10 minutes. Gums will start to pinken up, breathing will deepen and heartbeat will strengthen. If not improving, repeat *Shock formula* and work with him another 10 minutes. When not out of shock in half an hour, consult vet immediately. With a head injury vet should always check for concussion even if the dog recovers quickly. Confine him to warm, quiet bed to rest and sleep.

SHOCK FORMULA—Put 4 tbsp. of rock candy in a small screw-topped jar, add 3 tbsp. brandy or whiskey and cover jar with waxed paper to prevent lid from sticking. Screw lid on tightly and shake jar over a period of several days to melt candy. If candy does not melt, add more brandy. If appears to be thin, add more candy. When formula is ready it is the thickness of heavy syrup. Store in refrigerator and carry bottle with dropper when you are traveling. For an emergency formula, mix 1 tsp. honey

First Aid and Glossary

105

or sugar with 1 tsp. brandy and 1 tsp. hot water. Dissolve and use as above. For some reason this works on Yorkies, even though people will tell you that alcohol should not be used in case of shock. My vet has saved other breeds with it and keeps it on hand. Thanks go to Goldie Stone for telling us about this many years ago.

SHORT-COUPLED—Same as cobby or close-coupled body.

SHOULDER OUT—Loose muscles permit shoulder to slip out at joint.

SNIPEY FACE—Face too sharp-pointed and narrow. Not desirable in Yorkies.

SORE RECTUM—For simple redness or soreness from feces sticking to rectum, bathe with warm water and apply thin coat of vaseline or Benzocaine ointment.

SPLAY FOOT—Widespread toes and foot. Toes not tightly fit together. A fault in any breed.

STIFLE—Joint inside hind leg. Same as knee joint on humans. Separates second thigh from upper thigh. Often called, in error, patella or kneecap. Patella is a bone and stifle is a joint.

STING (by ant, bee or wasp)—If stinger remains in dog pull out with tweezers. Mix 1 tsp. baking soda with 1 pt. water. Bathe affected parts with solution. If this does not help, apply vinegar on cotton or Benzocaine ointment. When bite is on throat, it is very dangerous. If throat or tongue swells, call vet immediately. A dog can be allergic to the poison in these stings just as a human can. Usually dog improves in minutes.

SWAYBACK—Back is concave and sways down in middle. Opposite of roachback.

TEETH—Keep clean by brushing with small brush and any good toothpaste, or buy tooth scaler at pet shop. Get puppy used to these things at an early age and keep tartar from teeth to preserve them.

TEMPERATURE—Normal is considered to be 101° to 101.6°. Use rectal thermometer. Coat tip with vaseline and gently insert into rectum. Hold dog firmly and keep thermometer inside dog for 3 minutes.

TRANQUILIZERS—Never use unless vet prescribes, and then in exact amount prescribed. Dangerous to Yorkies.

TRUE THIGH—Also called upper thigh, thigh proper or first thigh. Located from rump down to stifle joint.

UNDERSHOT MOUTH—Lower teeth protrude beyond upper teeth. A fault.

WARNING SIGNS (of a sick dog)—Consult your vet immediately for:

1. Any *complete* change from normal behavior occurring for several days. This way you may catch a problem when it starts.

2. Limpness and listlessness if the dog is feverish. Check temperature.

3. Refusal of food and water for more than one day or if he drinks excessive amounts of water and takes no food.

4. Whimpering and definite signs of pain that you can't locate.

5. Vomiting if it is prolonged. Mild stomach upsets will cause a dog to vomit foamy, yellow liquid a few times and then he improves. This is normal. Watch diet for too much fat or sweets. A dog can regurgitate at will when he eats something he does not like or want. Also normal, but happens when he eats and food is intact. But when vomiting is prolonged to the stage where he is dry-retching, something is wrong.

6. When you find him unconscious and do not know what happened. Brain damage can occur if he is not treated immediately.

WORMS—If worms are suspected, always have your vet check a sample of the dog's stool microscopically. There are many kinds of worms, and worm medicine is strong and dangerous. Probably more tiny dogs are killed by worm medicine than by worms. Scooting across the floor to scratch his rectum is more often a sign of anal glands being full than a sign of worms.